Cambridge Elements

Elements in Islam and the Sciences
edited by
Nidhal Guessoum
American University of Sharjah, United Arab Emirates
Stefano Bigliardi
Al Akhawayn University in Ifrane, Morocco

ISLAM AND MODERN COSMOLOGY

Enis Doko
Ibn Haldun University

Shaftesbury Road, Cambridge CB2 8EA, United Kingdom

One Liberty Plaza, 20th Floor, New York, NY 10006, USA

477 Williamstown Road, Port Melbourne, VIC 3207, Australia

314–321, 3rd Floor, Plot 3, Splendor Forum, Jasola District Centre,
New Delhi – 110025, India

103 Penang Road, #05–06/07, Visioncrest Commercial, Singapore 238467

Cambridge University Press is part of Cambridge University Press & Assessment,
a department of the University of Cambridge.

We share the University's mission to contribute to society through the pursuit of
education, learning and research at the highest international levels of excellence.

www.cambridge.org
Information on this title: www.cambridge.org/9781009608336

DOI: 10.1017/9781009608350

© Enis Doko 2026

This publication is in copyright. Subject to statutory exception and to the provisions
of relevant collective licensing agreements, no reproduction of any part may take
place without the written permission of Cambridge University Press & Assessment.

When citing this work, please include a reference to the DOI 10.1017/9781009608350

First published 2026

A catalogue record for this publication is available from the British Library

ISBN 978-1-009-60833-6 Hardback
ISBN 978-1-009-60834-3 Paperback
ISSN 2754-7094 (online)
ISSN 2754-7086 (print)

Cambridge University Press & Assessment has no responsibility for the persistence
or accuracy of URLs for external or third-party internet websites referred to in this
publication and does not guarantee that any content on such websites is, or will remain,
accurate or appropriate.

For EU product safety concerns, contact us at Calle de José Abascal, 56, 1°, 28003
Madrid, Spain, or email eugpsr@cambridge.org

Islam and Modern Cosmology

Elements in Islam and the Sciences

DOI: 10.1017/9781009608350
First published online: January 2026

Enis Doko
Ibn Haldun University

Author for correspondence: Enis Doko, enisdoko@gmail.com

Abstract: *Islam and Modern Cosmology* examines how contemporary cosmological theories intersect with Islamic theology, exploring how modern science and Islamic thought can be brought into meaningful dialogue. It begins with a concise overview of modern cosmology, followed by an exploration of the Qur'an's cosmological perspectives and the philosophical models of creation proposed by Muslim thinkers, comparing these ideas with current scientific understandings. The discussion then considers the fine-tuning argument for God's existence and addresses the multiverse hypothesis, proposing that, under certain reasonable assumptions, the Islamic conception of God suggests the possibility of multiple universes. Finally, from a Muslim – specifically Sufi – perspective, it reflects on the problem of the significance of human life within this vast cosmos.

Keywords: Islamic cosmology, multiverse, fine-tuning argument, creation of the universe in Islam, Islam and science

© Enis Doko 2026

ISBNs: 9781009608336 (HB), 9781009608343 (PB), 9781009608350 (OC)
ISSNs: 2754-7094 (online), 2754-7086 (print)

Contents

1 Contemporary Cosmology in a Nutshell — 1

2 Creation and Cosmos: Islamic Theology Meets Modern Cosmology — 10

3 Divine Precision: Fine-Tuning and Islamic Theology — 28

4 Lord of the Worlds: Exploring the Multiverse in an Islamic Context — 48

5 The Way of Love: Human Significance in a Vast Universe — 62

References — 68

1 Contemporary Cosmology in a Nutshell

Physical cosmology, in contrast to metaphysical or religious cosmologies (such as Islamic cosmology), is the scientific study of the universe as a whole. It focuses on the universe's large-scale structure, including its origins, evolution, and ultimate fate. While metaphysical or religious cosmologies explore the universe from philosophical or spiritual perspectives, physical cosmology relies on observations, mathematical tools, simulations, and physical models. These tools are crucial in understanding the universe's dynamics and composition and underpinning the scientific rigor of the field. I will reserve the term "cosmology" for physical cosmology unless stated otherwise in this Element.

1.1 The Vastness of the Universe

The universe is unimaginably vast. We do not know its exact size, but the observable universe, the portion of the entire universe that we can see or detect from Earth, is over 93 billion light-years in diameter. This limit is set by the finite speed of light and the age of the universe. Anything beyond this boundary is neither observable nor detectable (so while it likely exists, we have no observational access to it). A light-year is the distance that light travels in a vacuum for one year, approximately 9.46 trillion kilometers, and the observable universe is roughly 93 billion light-years in diameter.

The observable universe contains hundreds of billions of galaxies, each composed of millions to trillions of stars, planets, and other celestial objects. These galaxies are not randomly distributed but are organized into larger structures known as galaxy clusters and superclusters. Between these clusters are immense voids, vast regions of empty space where very few galaxies reside. Beyond these, on the largest scales, the universe forms a web-like structure known as the cosmic web, composed of filaments of galaxies.

The Earth is a tiny speck in this vast cosmic arena, orbiting an ordinary star in a relatively unremarkable corner of a single galaxy among trillions. We will ponder our place in this immensity further in our final section.

1.2 The Road to the Big Bang Model

For centuries, many philosophers believed the universe was eternal and unchanging. This view began to shift in the early twentieth century, when Albert Einstein (1879–1955) formulated the general theory of relativity in 1915 – a more comprehensive theory of gravity than Isaac Newton's (1642–1727). While Einstein initially sought a static solution, the equations themselves implied that the cosmos could not remain static – it must expand or contract.

To preserve the idea of a static universe, Einstein introduced a "cosmological constant" (Λ). However, after Edwin Hubble's 1929 discovery of the universe's expansion, Einstein reportedly called the constant his "biggest blunder," as it had masked the dynamic nature of his own equations – a possibility first explored by Alexander Friedmann (1888–1925) in the early 1920s.

In the 1920s, Alexander Friedmann found dynamic solutions to Einstein's equations, describing an expanding universe. However, his work remained largely unknown at the time and lacked observational support. In 1929, Edwin Hubble (1889–1953) discovered that distant galaxies are receding from us – the farther away a galaxy is, the faster it moves away. This relationship, now known as Hubble's Law, provided the first strong empirical evidence for cosmic expansion, in line with Friedmann's theoretical model. Building on these developments, in 1931 Georges Lemaître (1894–1966) proposed that the universe expanded from a "primeval atom," a hypothesis that laid the groundwork for what would later be called the Big Bang theory.

While expansion was groundbreaking, it didn't immediately settle debates about the universe's origin. In the late 1940s, George Gamow (1904–1968), with Ralph Alpher (1921–2007) and Robert Herman (1914–1997), proposed that a hot, dense early universe would leave behind residual thermal radiation. This prediction came true in 1965, when Arno Penzias (1933–2024) and Robert Wilson (b. 1936) accidentally detected the cosmic microwave background (CMB), a faint glow from the early universe. This discovery was a major confirmation of the Big Bang model, earning Penzias and Wilson the Nobel Prize.[1]

1.3 Hot Big Bang Model

Einstein's General Theory of Relativity, when combined with the cosmological principle and assumptions about the matter content of the universe, leads to a family of solutions known as the Friedmann equations. These equations govern how the universe evolves over time under the assumption that it is homogeneous and isotropic on large scales. The cosmological principle, which underlies these models, posits that the universe is homogeneous and isotropic when viewed on sufficiently large scales. This principle is empirically supported: surveys such as the Sloan Digital Sky Survey (SDSS) and the 2dF Galaxy Redshift Survey reveal that, although galaxies form clusters and voids on small scales, the distribution becomes statistically uniform on scales larger

---

[1] A highly accessible and engaging account of the Big Bang theory's history that readers can consult is (Singh, 2005). For more academic overviews of the history of cosmology, including Big Bang Theory, readers can consult (Kragh, 2007) and (North, 2008).

than 300 million light-years. Similarly, measurements of the cosmic microwave background (CMB) from COBE, WMAP, and Planck show remarkable isotropy, with temperature fluctuations of only one part in 100,000. These observations justify the use of the cosmological principle in building simplified but powerful cosmological models, such as those based on the Friedmann equations.[2]

When we apply the Friedmann solutions in reverse – tracing the universe's expansion backward in time – we always find that the universe contracts, becoming denser and hotter. As we approach earlier moments, the equations predict that density and temperature increase without bound. Extrapolating all the way back leads to a theoretical state of infinite density, temperature, and space-time curvature: a singularity. This singularity marks the breakdown of general relativity and the beginning of what we call the Big Bang, which is estimated in various ways to have occurred about 13.8 billion years ago.

The term "Big Bang" is used in two different ways by cosmologists and philosophers, which sometimes leads to confusion. Some physicists refer to the Big Bang as the moment of singularity. This identifies the universe's origin as a point of infinite density, temperature, and space-time curvature. In this framework, the singularity marks the beginning of the universe, which we cannot describe using conventional physics. Some thinkers interpret the singularity as nothing. Other scientists define the Big Bang not as the singularity but as the point when the universe was at or near Planck density. Planck density is about 10^{93} grams per cubic centimeter (a billion galaxies in the volume of an atomic nucleus). This would be the density at 10^{-43} seconds after the singularity, called the Planck epoch, which refers to the earliest period in the universe's history when quantum effects and gravitational effects were equally strong.

I prefer to adopt the second definition in this Element because I want to differentiate between empirically well-established science and unverified speculation. While general relativity works exceptionally well on large scales, it does not incorporate quantum mechanics, which becomes crucial at extremely small scales and high energies. At the Planck epoch, quantum effects can no longer be ignored. Hence, we need a new theory incorporating both quantum physics and general relativity. While some proposals exist, such as string theory and loop quantum gravity, there is currently no well-established quantum theory of gravity. Therefore, the singularity should be interpreted as an outcome of extrapolating general relativity beyond its domain of validity.

---

[2] For a nontechnical, yet detailed, discussion of the Big Bang model and cosmology, readers may consult (Perlov & Vilenkin, 2017). For an undergraduate-level introduction to cosmology, one can consult (Ryden, 2017). For a more advanced discussion of cosmology, I highly recommend (Mukhanov, 2005).

1.4 Brief History of the Early Universe

As the universe expanded, its temperature dropped, driving major transitions. In the extremely hot moments after the Big Bang, only fundamental particles existed. According to the standard model of particle physics, twelve fundamental particles of matter exist – three of which (electrons, up quarks, and down quarks) combined to form atoms. These particles were being created and destroyed rapidly.

At a hundred-billionth of a second, the universe reached quadrillion degrees. This marked the electroweak phase transition, during which the electromagnetic force (governing interactions between charged particles) and the weak nuclear force (responsible for radioactive decay) – once unified – separated into distinct forces.

By a hundred-thousandth of a second, the universe had cooled enough for only stable particles such as quarks and electrons to persist. These quarks would eventually combine into the first composite particles – protons and neutrons. Particle collisions during this epoch were extremely energetic, similar to those recreated today in high-energy particle accelerators like the Large Hadron Collider.

Each particle has an antiparticle of opposite charge. For example, electrons have positrons. When a particle meets its antiparticle, they annihilate, producing radiation/energy. In the early universe, equal amounts of matter and antimatter were produced, but due to a slight asymmetry – possibly involving CP violation – a small excess of matter remained. As the universe cooled, radiation had low energy (thus little particle-antiparticle creation occurred), and annihilation processes dominated. Antiprotons and antineutrons vanished within a second. By 10 seconds, most positrons were gone. The surviving matter formed all the stars and galaxies.

Free neutrons decay into protons with a half-life of about 10 minutes, while protons are stable. Initially, equal numbers existed, but while free neutrons decayed and the universe cooled, fusion began. Around one minute after the Big Bang, protons and neutrons formed deuterium, then helium-3 and helium-4. This Big Bang nucleosynthesis ended within 20 minutes, producing hydrogen, helium, and trace lithium – insufficient for life, but stars would later resume nucleosynthesis.

Approximately 370,000 years after the Big Bang, the universe cooled to about 4,000 degrees, allowing electrons to bond with nuclei, forming neutral atoms – a phase called recombination. Before this, free electrons scattered light, rendering the universe opaque. After recombination, light traveled freely, ultimately becoming the cosmic microwave background radiation that fills the whole universe, now a key pillar of Big Bang evidence.

1.5 Formation of Galaxies and Stars

After recombination, the universe entered the "Dark Ages," lasting tens of millions of years without new light. It was filled with neutral hydrogen and helium and remained mostly uniform, with slight density variations. Gravity amplified these variations, pulling matter into denser clumps surrounded by voids.

This clumping was driven primarily by dark matter, which interacts only via gravity and does not emit light. Although we cannot directly observe it, dark matter's gravitational effects on galaxies and stars indicate it comprises about 27 percent of the universe's total mass-energy.[3]

Over tens of millions of years, regions gathered enough mass that cosmic expansion no longer prevented (local) collapse. These early structures – smaller than today's galaxies – grew by merging and accreting matter. Dark matter, which made up 90 percent of their mass, dominated their formation, while hydrogen and helium constituted the rest.

Within these protogalaxies, gas concentrated more tightly than dark matter because it could cool and collapse via electromagnetic interactions. Dark matter, unable to radiate energy, remained diffuse. As gas collapsed and heated, core temperatures reached about 15 million degrees – igniting nuclear fusion and forming the first stars. Fusion occurs when lighter nuclei like hydrogen merge into heavier elements such as helium, releasing energy. It powers stars and produces heat and light.

The first stars likely formed 30–200 million years after the Big Bang. They were massive – up to 200 times the Sun's mass – and short-lived. These early stars burned their fuel quickly and exploded as supernovae, ejecting elements like carbon and oxygen into space. Their remnants likely became black holes.

Second-generation stars, formed from enriched material, were smaller and longer-lived. Our Sun, a third-generation star, formed 5 billion years ago from the material produced by earlier stars. Except for hydrogen and helium, all atoms on Earth originated from those first-generation stars. Thus, star formation is essential for the chemistry that enables life.

1.6 The Theory of Cosmic Inflation

Observational evidence strongly supports the Hot Big Bang Model, and cosmologists widely accept it. As Yacov Zel'dovich stated, "I am as sure of the Big

---

[3] For a detailed discussion of dark mater see: (Freeman & McNamara (2006).

Bang as I am that the Earth goes around the Sun" (Perlov & Vilenkin, 2017: 344). Still, the model has limitations. It does not explain several important features of the universe. The Theory of Cosmic Inflation was developed to address these gaps.

Three major problems challenge the Big Bang Model. First is the Horizon Problem: observations show that the cosmic microwave background (CMB) is nearly uniform across vast distances, despite those regions being too far apart to have exchanged information or energy. This uniformity in "causally disconnected" regions is puzzling.

Second is the Flatness Problem: the universe appears nearly flat, that is, well described by Euclidean geometry. According to Friedmann's solutions, any slight early deviation from flatness would have grown significantly over time. Yet, observations show almost perfect flatness, implying that the universe started with extremely fine-tuned conditions.

The third issue is the Magnetic Monopole Problem. Grand Unified Theories (GUTs) predict the creation of magnetic monopoles – hypothetical particles with a single magnetic pole – during the Big Bang. These should be abundant, yet none have been observed. Their absence contradicts expectations.

Cosmic Inflation solves these problems. It proposes a brief period of rapid, exponential expansion just after the Big Bang, enlarging distances by a factor of $10^{26}-10^{30}$ in a very brief fraction of a second.

Inflation explains the Horizon Problem because regions now far apart were once close enough to equilibrate before expansion pushed them apart. It resolves the Flatness Problem by stretching space so uniformly that any initial curvature becomes undetectable. It also explains the lack of monopoles by diluting their density to negligible levels.

In the late 1970s, Alan Guth and others studied scalar fields – energy fields in space-time – and found that a universe dominated by such a field could expand rapidly. This rapid expansion phase is what we call inflation. The energy from the scalar field drove inflation, and as it decayed into particles, the universe transitioned to the more gradual expansion of the Hot Big Bang phase.

Guth's model had issues with non-uniformities after inflation (Guth, 1981). Andrei Linde later improved it by proposing that the inflationary regions were vastly larger than the observable universe, preserving uniformity (Linde, 1983).

Inflation not only explains the early universe's smoothness and flatness but also accounts for the small fluctuations in density that seeded the formation of cosmic structures. These predictions are supported by observations. Inflation remains the leading theory of the universe's earliest moments.[4]

1.7 Eternal Inflation and Multiverse

Inflation occurs when a region of the universe contains high energy in a scalar field, causing rapid, massive expansion. After a fraction of a second, the scalar field decays into particles, and the universe expands at a slower rate, as described by the original Big Bang model.

Due to quantum fluctuations, inflation may last slightly longer in some regions. In the scenario known as eternal inflation, while inflation ends in some areas, it continues in others. This leads to an ever-expanding space filled with, according to the theory, "bubbles" – post-inflationary regions – embedded in still-inflating space. Our observable universe is, again according to the theory, just one such bubble.[5]

Eternal inflation challenges the idea of a singular Big Bang. Each bubble begins with near-uniform conditions, flat geometry, and sufficient energy to form matter. These bubbles evolve like our universe, forming stars and possibly life. Meanwhile, inflation continues elsewhere, generating new bubbles indefinitely.

As an inflating region grows, more bubbles form – each moment producing exponentially more bubbles than the last. This means that most of the bubbles existing now are the ones that formed in the last fraction of a second, making our 13.8-billion-year-old bubble seem ancient by comparison.

Different bubbles may exhibit different physical laws, depending on local scalar field values. For instance, the Higgs field sets particle masses in our universe; other scalar fields could produce different physics in other bubbles.

These bubbles are often referred to as separate "universes," with the entire inflating structure termed the "multiverse." While the "observable universe" includes everything we can detect, eternal inflation suggests a far larger, possibly infinite multiverse.

Whether eternal inflation is real remains uncertain. Theoretical physics supports it, and one potential observational signature would be evidence of a bubble collision, detectable as a circular anomaly in the cosmic background radiation.

1.8 String Theory, Branes, and Cosmic Landscape

String theory proposes that all matter is composed of tiny one-dimensional strings. Different vibrational patterns of these strings correspond to different

---

[4] For a detailed discussion of the inflation theory, readers can consult the book written by the scientist who developed the theory (Guth, 1997).

[5] For an accessible exposition of eternal inflation see (Linde, 1994).

particles, including the graviton, the hypothetical quantum carrier of gravity. String theory seeks to unify the Standard Model of particle physics with General Relativity.[6] However, it requires six additional spatial dimensions beyond the three we observe. To explain why we don't detect these additional dimensions, theorists propose two models: branes and compact dimensions.

A useful analogy comes from the novel *Flatland: A Romance of Many Dimensions (1884)* by Edwin A. Abbott (1838–1926), a story of beings in a 2D world, unaware of a third dimension. Similarly, we may live on a 3D "brane" embedded in higher-dimensional space. In these braneworld models, particles – including light – are confined to the brane, making extra dimensions undetectable. Other branes could exist nearby, perhaps mere millionths of a meter away in a higher dimension, but remain invisible because we cannot interact with them.

In the 9D universe suggested by string theory, branes of various dimensions (from one to eight) populate the cosmos. Each brane constitutes its own universe. Some may have undergone inflation and Big Bang-like expansion, just like ours.

In compact dimension models, extra dimensions are tightly curled up, like the circular cross-section of a straw. Creatures living on the surface would perceive only one dimension unless they could probe extremely small scales. Likewise, string theory's extra dimensions are thought to be curled up near the Planck length, far beyond current detection capabilities.

A combination of eternal inflation and braneworld theory suggests there could be countless branes, each undergoing its own inflation and creating separate bubbles. Depending on their structure and dimensions, different branes could have different particles and physical laws.

These compact dimensions influence the properties of strings, affecting particle masses and force strengths. There are countless ways to "compactify" them, creating different vacuum states. This collection is called the string theory landscape. Combined with inflation, the string theory landscape suggests a multiverse: different regions of space settle into different vacuum states, each with its own physical laws. While string theory remains untested due to its high energy scale, it provides a theoretical foundation for this multiverse view.[7]

1.9 Dark Energy and the Future of the Universe

The universe is expanding, with most galaxies moving away from each other. While stars in our galaxy and nearby galaxies are bound by gravity, distant

---

[6] For an accessible and fun read on String theory see (Greene, 1999). For a mathematical but basic introduction to String Theory one can consult (Zwiebach, 2009). For a detailed discussion of higher dimensions and their role in modern physics see (Randall, 2005).

[7] For further reading about string theory landscape see (Susskind, 2005).

galaxies continue to recede. Over trillions of years, stars will burn out – small ones becoming white dwarfs and larger ones collapsing into neutron stars or black holes. New stars will form from leftover gas and dust, but eventually the hydrogen needed for star formation will run out, leaving galaxies as dark collections of cooling stars.

The future depends on whether the universe's expansion continues or reverses, which is influenced by the forces driving galaxies apart. Though we do not know what started the expansion 13.8 billion years ago, inflation briefly accelerated it, and galaxies continue to move apart due to their inertia.

Gravity, which works between all objects in the universe, pulls galaxies back toward each other. As galaxies move apart, gravity tries to slow this expansion. If galaxies move fast enough, they'll keep separating forever; if not, they'll eventually fall back toward each other, similar to how a thrown ball either falls back or escapes Earth's gravity, depending on its speed.

The outcome depends on the universe's density and how fast galaxies are moving. A higher density means a stronger gravitational pull, requiring galaxies to move faster to avoid re-collapse. Current measurements show that the universe's density is within 1 percent of the threshold, making it unclear whether galaxies will eventually fall back or expand forever. Einstein's theory predicts that infinite universes expand forever while finite ones re-collapse, but we cannot yet determine which scenario applies to our universe. Either way, the universe will likely continue expanding for trillions of years.

In the 1970s, the fate of the universe seemed clear: if above critical density, it would collapse into a "big crunch"; if below, it would drift into an eternal "heat death," where particles and radiation spread out indefinitely (with no usable energy). We could not tell which was true.

Inflation changed that by explaining why the universe remains so close to critical density. During inflation, the universe moved closer to this value, reaching near-perfect critical density. Unfortunately, this means we can't measure if the universe is slightly above or below the critical density, as both scenarios would look identical for a very long time (whether it re-collapses or expands forever).

The discovery of dark energy in the 1990s changed our understanding of the universe's future. Dark energy pushes galaxies apart faster, opposing gravity.[8] Astronomers found that for the last five billion years, galaxies have been accelerating away from each other. Currently, about two-thirds of the universe's energy is dark energy, which suggests the universe is headed toward heat death, expanding forever.

---

[8] For more information about dark energy see chapter 11 of (Nicolson, 2007) and (Clegg, 2019).

In a universe dominated by dark energy, critical density does not affect its long-term fate – dark energy will cause endless expansion. However, since we do not fully understand dark energy, there's a possibility it could decay into regular matter (as has happened before). During inflation, the universe expanded rapidly due to a scalar field exerting repulsive gravity. Scalar fields decayed into matter, which slowed down expansion after inflation. Billions of years later, dark energy took over, causing the universe to accelerate again, though not as rapidly as inflation.

If dark energy decays, gravity could dominate, and the universe's fate would once again depend on whether we are above or below critical density. If above, the universe could eventually re-collapse. If dark energy persists forever, the universe will continue expanding endlessly.

One leading theory suggests that dark energy might be like scalar fields during inflation: dark energy will eventually decay into matter, altering the universe's fate. Another theory, however, proposes that dark energy is an intrinsic property of space, meaning it would never change, and the universe will continue expanding toward a heat death.[9]

This concludes our summary of contemporary, scientific cosmology. We are ready to examine Islamic religious cosmology and compare it with scientific cosmology.

2 Creation and Cosmos: Islamic Theology Meets Modern Cosmology

2.1 Mere Islam

Islam is a monotheistic faith that worships a single, all-powerful deity commonly referred to as *Allah*, which translates to "The God." It is the world's second-largest religion, with over 1.8 billion followers spanning various cultures and regions, including the Middle East, the Balkans, North Africa, South Asia, and Southeast Asia, with expanding communities in Europe, the Americas, and sub-Saharan Africa. It is one of the three principal Abrahamic religions, alongside Judaism and Christianity, sharing a common heritage and analogous beliefs.

Like any major religious tradition, Islam encompasses various sects and interpretations. Although I am a follower of the *Ḥanafī-Māturīdī* School within Sunni Islam, which represents the largest branch of Islam, I will adopt a nonsectarian approach in this Element. Like C. S. Lewis's (1898–1963) concept of *Mere Christianity* (2001), I will discuss "Mere Islam," referring to

---

[9] For more detailed discussion of the future of the universe consult the relevant chapters of (Adams & Laughlin, 1999).

the fundamental beliefs common to all Islamic denominations. Lewis describes "Mere Christianity" as the foundational beliefs shared broadly among Christians, akin to a shared hallway leading to rooms representing different denominations.

Fortunately, I need not invent my definition of "Mere Islam." Muslim scholastic theologians, often known as *Mutakallimūn*, who practiced *Kalam* (i.e., Muslim Theology), have articulated a concise definition. They summarized the core beliefs shared by all Islamic sects under *al-Uṣūl al-Thalātha* ("The Three Principles") (Yavuz, 2012). Let us explore these principles.

The first principle, *Ulūhiyyah* or Godhead, asserts a strictly monotheistic concept of God as outlined in the doctrine of *Tawḥīd*, which underscores God's absolute singularity. God is ubiquitous, incomparable, and without equal or partner, omnipotent, omniscient, and merciful. *Ulūhiyyah* rejects any form of anthropomorphism or division in God, including the Christian doctrines of the Trinity and the divinity of Jesus.

The second principle, *Nubuwwah* or Prophethood, holds that God communicated with humanity through a succession of prophets. Muslims believe that prophets, virtuous individuals bestowed with divine revelations, have been sent to every nation (although not all their names are known). Prophets exemplify and teach Islam's principles, affirm God's oneness, and guide their communities toward ethical and spiritual integrity. The prophetic line begins with Adam and culminates with Muhammad, the final prophet, whose revelations are recorded in the Qur'an. The Qur'an, written in Classical Arabic, is regarded as the verbatim word of God and the primary source of Islamic theology and law. Alongside the Qur'an, the Hadith – sayings and actions of the Prophet Muhammad – play a crucial role in Islamic theology. However, while all agree on the content and authority of the Qur'an, there is disagreement regarding the authenticity of certain hadiths.

The third principle, *ākhirah* or afterlife, posits life as a trial in preparation for the afterlife, where God resurrects and judges individuals. The afterlife comprises Paradise and Hell, where souls are rewarded or punished based on earthly deeds. The Day of Judgment involves a detailed reckoning of each person's actions, ensuring ultimate justice.

The first and second principles are particularly relevant to discussions at the intersection of cosmology and Islam. The notions that God is the creator of the universe and that the Qur'an is the literal word of God suggest that Qur'anic cosmology is pivotal to our understanding of Islam's perspective on cosmology. We will delve into these issues, beginning with an overview of the cosmological perspective presented in the Qur'an, but first, we will discuss the epistemology of Islamic theology.

2.2 Sources of Knowledge in the Islamic Tradition

The *mutakallimūn*, Islamic theologians engaged in scholastic theology (*kalām*), agree on three valid sources of knowledge: reason, sense perception, and testimony.[10]

Reason enables us to evaluate necessary, possible, and impossible propositions and to move from sensory observations to more abstract or theoretical conclusions, including conclusions about realities that are not observable. According to the *mutakallimūn*, reason is an essential and self-evident faculty. They argue that even denying the validity of reason entails a contradiction, since such a denial would itself require the use of reason. While some theological schools, such as the *Salafī* movement, accept reason in practical and empirical domains, they argue that it should not be the basis of theological conclusions, especially where scriptural texts are concerned. However, the *mutakallimūn* maintain that reason is indispensable even in theology, and they find support in the Qur'an, which repeatedly invites both believers and skeptics to reflect and reason about the world, life, and divine truths.

Sense perception is considered indispensable because most knowledge comes directly from the senses or through reason based on sensory experience. While the senses can sometimes mislead us, all knowledge about the physical world originates from them.

Testimony refers to knowledge gained from others about events we have not witnessed. Although testimony is generally seen as less reliable than reason and sense perception due to potential deception, testimony is essential for religious knowledge. Divine revelation and the life and teachings of the Prophet Muhammad (the *Sunnah*) are known through testimonial reports.

There are two types of testimony: multiple or mass reports and singular reports. Multiple testimonies come from numerous independent and trustworthy narrators, making falsehood unlikely; such reports are considered highly reliable. The Qur'an and parts of the *Sunnah* fall into this category according to the *mutakallimūn*.

Since science is a product of the sophisticated use of reason and sense perception, scientific results should be taken as reliable sources of knowledge for theological discussion.

We should note that a minority Muslim group, the *Salafīs*, prioritize the Qur'an and *Sunnah* over theological reasoning (*kalām*) and philosophical inquiry, which they often regard as unwarranted innovations (*bid'ah*) or as harmful deviations from revealed knowledge.

---

[10] For a more detailed review of Islamic Epistemology, readers may consult (Doko & Turner, 2023: 148–162).

2.3 The Qur'an's Cosmology

Physical cosmology aims to explain how the universe works, focusing on natural laws and phenomena. It seeks to understand the physical mechanisms behind cosmic events. While the Qur'an contains verses referencing the creation of the heavens and the earth, celestial bodies, and other cosmological phenomena, it has a different aim. It tries to emphasize the Principle of *Tawḥīd* of Islam as well as God's power and wisdom in creating and sustaining the universe. Unlike the physical sciences, the Qur'an seeks to convey spiritual truths and moral guidance. The Qur'an emphasizes the relationship between the Creator and the creation, highlighting themes like purpose, destiny, and the meaning of human existence. We should consider this difference in aim when studying scripture and scientific cosmology.[11]

Unlike the Bible's detailed description in Genesis 1–3, the Qur'an does not provide a chronology or details of the creation of the universe. However, several verses in the Qur'an, scattered through different chapters, refer to the creation of the universe. In this section, we will look at those verses.

Like the Bible, the Qur'an frequently mentions that God created the heavens and the earth in six days. However, the Qur'an does not accept the Biblical account as an accurate description, explicitly denying the claim that God rested on the seventh day (Genesis 2:2–3):

> And We [God] certainly created the heavens and the earth and what is between them in six days, and there touched Us no weariness. (*Qāf* 50:38)

The Arabic word used in the Qur'an for "day" is *yawm*. In Arabic, *yawm* denotes different lengths of time, such as "24-hour day," "longer or shorter periods than 24 hours," and "extended duration" (such as an era or a phase in history) (Karaman et al., 2020: vol. 5, 112–113). In cosmological and metaphysical cases, the Qur'an itself uses "day" in the sense of more extended periods:

> And they ask you to hasten the punishment. But Allah will never fail in His promise. And indeed, a day with your Lord is like a thousand years of those which you count. (*al-Ḥajj* 22:47)

> The angels and the Spirit ascend to Him in a day, the measure of which is fifty thousand years. (*al-Maʿārij* 70:4)

We will not try to determine the exact interpretation of *yawm* in the context of the six days of creation. Suffice it to say that the Qur'an's flexible use of *yawm* allows for interpretations that accommodate scientific findings.

---

[11] For an insightful analysis of the Qur'an's cosmology as well as Islamic attitudes toward cosmology, see Guessoum, 2011: 179–193.

Another Qur'anic verse relevant to the creation of the universe is *al-Anbiyā'* (21:30):

> Have those who disbelieved not considered that the heavens and the earth were a joined entity, and We separated them and made from water every living thing? Then will they not believe? (*al-Anbiyā'* 21:30)

The critical terms in the aforementioned verse are *ratq* and *fataq*. The term *ratq* refers to something closed up, fused together, or in a state of union without any separation or fissure. It conveys the idea of being tightly knit or compacted. On the other hand, *fataq* means to split, separate, cleave asunder, or cause to burst open. It implies an action of breaking apart something that was previously unified.

Some contemporary Muslim *tafsīr* (Qur'anic exegesis) scholars, such as Muhammad Asad (1900–1992) (Esed, 2002: 650–651) and Mehmet Okuyan (1965) (Okuyan, 2024: 795), interpret the aforementioned verse as aligning with the modern Big Bang model of the universe, which we studied in the previous section. It is important to note that scientific models or theories are complex mathematical structures that cannot be summarized in a single sentence. This applies to the Big Bang theory as well. Therefore, we should not expect to find a single verse in the Qur'an that encapsulates a physical theory.

While some contemporary scholars see thematic resonance between this verse and modern cosmology, particularly in its description of an initial unity and subsequent separation, it is important to be cautious in drawing strong conclusions. The verse refers to both the heavens and the Earth as a unified entity, whereas in modern cosmology, the Earth formed billions of years after the initial cosmic expansion. This temporal gap complicates any direct alignment between the verse and the Big Bang model.

Basil Altaie (1952) is more cautious, pointing to the presence of heavy elements such as uranium in our solar system, he notes that "heaven and earth" may refer not to the initial cosmic singularity but to a later nebular cloud which split into distinct bodies (Altaie, 2019: 179). In this reading, the verse would pertain to a specific phase in the formation of our solar system rather than the origin of the entire cosmos, offering a more temporally and materially grounded interpretation.

Nevertheless, it is worth noting that many early Muslim scholars[12] interpreted the verse as indicating that the heavens and the Earth were originally joined in a single mass, later separated by God. This shows that such

---

[12] Such as 'Abdullāh ibn 'Abbās (619–687), Abū Qatādah al-Anṣārī (584–656), Ad-Daḥḥāk ibn Muzāḥim (d. 723), and Al-Ḥasan al-Baṣrī (642–728) (Öztürk, 2015: 71).

interpretations predate modern cosmology and are not simply retroactive attempts to read science into scripture.

Some classical scholars[13] offered an alternative interpretation: the "joining" refers to the earth being barren and the sky withholding rain, while the "separation" refers to Allah sending rain to the earth, enabling life to flourish.

Another verse that is often related to the Big Bang model by contemporary *tafsīr* scholars is *adh-Dhāriyāt* (51:47):

> And the heaven We constructed with strength, and indeed, We are [its] expander. (*adh-Dhāriyāt* 51:47)

In this verse, the critical term is *mūsi'ūn*. Derived from *awsa'a*, meaning to expand or make wide, *mūsi'ūn* can be translated as "We are expanding" or "We are expanders." Classical *tafsīr* scholars have typically interpreted this statement metaphorically, referring to the abundant sustenance that Allah provides. Another metaphorical interpretation understands the expansion as a symbol of Allah's limitless power and authority (Nasr et al., 2015: 1278).

However, if taken literally, the verse suggests that the cosmos is expanding, which aligns with modern cosmological findings. Asad (Esed, 2002: 1070–1071) and Okuyan (Okuyan, 2024: 1279) also interpret the verse in this light. It is important to note, however, that this should not be seen as an explicit formulation of the Big Bang model, which is a complex scientific theory expressed through detailed mathematical structures and cannot be reduced to a single sentence. Rather, the verse can be understood as broadly consistent with the empirical observation of the universe's expansion.

Altaie underlines the literal force of the verb *mus'i'ūn*, linking it to contemporary work on the dark-energy-driven acceleration of the universe and contrasting it with the Aristotelian idea of a static sky (Altaie, 2019: 153–154). His reading emphasizes that the Qur'ān's language, when taken seriously, opens space for cosmological insight that diverge significantly from the dominant premodern cosmology, which saw the heavens as fixed and unchanging.

The third verse, which is connected with modern cosmology by contemporary scholars, is *Fuṣṣilat* (41:11):

> Then He directed Himself to the heaven while it was smoke and said to it and to the earth, "Come [into being], willingly or unwillingly." They said, "We have come willingly." (*Fuṣṣilat* 41:11)

The verse highlights Allah's authority over creation and its submission to His will, thereby reinforcing *Tawḥīd*. However, the term "smoke" has garnered

---

[13] Such as 'Ikrimah al-Barbarī (d. 723), 'Aṭiyyah ibn Sa'd (d. 710), 'Abd al-Raḥmān ibn Zayd (d. 798) and ibn Jarīr al-Ṭabarī (839–923) (Öztürk, 2015: 72; Karaman et al., 2020: vol. 3, 675–577)

significant attention. While the Arabic term *dukhān* generally means "smoke" resulting from combustion, it can also refer to mist or vapor, as it was used in pre-Islamic poetry (Karaman et al., 2020: vol. 4, 693–694).

Traditionally, the reference to smoke has been interpreted as describing the origin of the heavens, indicating a formless, vaporous state. Some contemporary scholars such as Asad (Esed, 2002: 971–972) and Okuyan (Okuyan, 2024: 1162) associate the verse with the Big Bang theory, arguing that the early universe was filled with hot gases such as hydrogen and helium. Altaie connects this "smoke" with the astrophysical picture of a proto-solar nebula rich in dust and gas, and correlates the Qur'an's seven-heavens motif with successive orbital shells of the young solar system, stressing that the image concerns local planetary evolution rather than the birth of the entire universe (Altaie, 2019: 179–181).

Another verse that has been attributed cosmological importance would, if taken literally, conflict with modern science is:

> And it is He who created the heavens and the earth in six days – and His Throne had been upon water – that He might test you as to which of you is best in deed. But if you say, "Indeed, you are resurrected after death," those who disbelieve will surely say, "This is not but obvious magic." (*Hūd* 11:7)

The main message of the aforementioned verse is that Allah is the ultimate authority over all creation, and life is a test to determine who excels in deeds. It aims to encourage ethical conduct, spiritual growth, and preparation for the afterlife. However, the phrase "and His Throne was upon water" has been the subject of extensive debate in a cosmological context. This part of the verse seems to suggest that Allah's Throne was upon water before the creation of the heavens and the earth. This raises two questions: What is meant by "Allah's Throne" and the "water" that existed before the universe?

The term *'arsh*, meaning "throne," can mean a seat of authority or dominion (Okuyan, 2024: 541). The term *al-mā'*, which literally means "the water," has also been subject to various interpretations.

Some scholars take the verse literally. In this case, the Throne is seen as an actual entity, though its exact nature is beyond human comprehension. Others, however, take a symbolic interpretation, viewing the Throne as a symbol of Allah's supreme sovereignty and authority over creation (Karaman et al., 2020: vol. 3, 151).

Under the literal reading, the verse implies that water existed before the earth and heavens were created, holding that God first created water. However, this interpretation would conflict with the well-established cosmological model discussed in the previous section: water, consisting of two hydrogen atoms and one oxygen atom, could not have been the first substance in the universe. Hydrogen, helium, and trace amounts of lithium were the first elements created.

Hydrogen nuclei formed within the first few minutes of the universe's existence, while oxygen was only possible later in the cores of stars. Stars formed 100–200 million years after the Big Bang and, through nuclear fusion, created heavier elements, including oxygen. These elements were released into space upon the stars' deaths, allowing water molecules to form in interstellar molecular clouds when hydrogen and oxygen combined. This likely occurred 500 million to 1 billion years after the Big Bang. Thus, water could not have been the first substance in the universe.

Alternatively, some scholars interpret the verse metaphorically, taking "water" to symbolize the initial plasma state of the universe, thus aligning the verse with modern cosmology. However, this interpretation stretches the meaning of "water." Others argue that "water" symbolizes the unformed potential from which Allah created the universe.

Altaie argues that both terms are best read biologically rather than cosmologically: the "Throne" stands for the organizing principle of life itself, while "water" designates the indispensable substrate of life; thus, the clause links creation with the ethical trial of humans (Altaie, 2019: 186).

Abu Muslim al-Isfahānī (d. 934) offered an interesting metaphorical interpretation. According to his reading, the reference to water emphasizes the awe-inspiring magnificence of Allah's power. While builders construct on solid ground to ensure stability, Allah created the heavens and the earth without any such need (underscoring His omnipotence). This interpretation aligns well with the symbolic reading of the Throne (Öztürk, 2015: 60).

In another metaphorical reading, Muhammad Asad suggests that the Throne of God's almightiness resting upon water symbolizes the process by which God initiated the emergence of life from water. He supports this interpretation with two arguments. First, he connects it to *al-Anbiyā'* (21:30), emphasizing the creation of living things from water. Second, he notes that the preceding verses mention living creatures, reinforcing his interpretation that the Throne upon water symbolizes the origin of life (Esed, 2002: 422–423).

We will refrain from selecting the right interpretation here. Suffice it to say that multiple interpretations of the verse exist, each carrying the same core theological and spiritual message – Allah is the ultimate authority over all creation, and life is a test to determine who excels in deeds – without conflicting with modern cosmology.

Another verse often associated with cosmology is the following:

> The Day when We will fold up the heaven like the folding of a [written] scroll for records. As We began the first creation, We will repeat it. [That is] a promise binding upon Us. Indeed, We will do it. (*al-Anbiyā'* 21:104)

This verse is commonly interpreted as a metaphorical depiction of Allah rolling up the heavens like scrolls, symbolizing His immense power. It parallels other verses – such as *al-Zumar* (39:67) – that emphasize Allah's act of creating the universe from nothing and His power to fold it back on the Day of Judgment. The "folding" can be understood either as the total destruction of the current universe or as its return to its primordial state before creation. This act will be followed by the emergence of a new world, prepared for the afterlife. The imagery in this verse closely resembles descriptions found in the Bible, particularly Isaiah 34:4 and Revelation 6:14.

Altaie interprets Qur'an 21:104 – "The Day when We will roll up the heavens like the rolling up of a scroll" – as a direct reference to a cosmic collapse, akin to the Big Crunch scenario proposed in theoretical cosmology. He argues that this verse clearly describes a return of the universe to its original state, implying a closed or oscillatory universe model. Although modern observations favor an accelerating universe, Altaie still offers scientific room for future collapse, supported by a model he and his student developed in which the universe, represented as a cylindrical sheet, collapses and rolls up in a manner consistent with the verse (Altaie, 2019: 157–158).

Nidhal Guessoum, however, is critical. While acknowledging that some scholars have drawn connections between this verse and the Big Crunch, he emphasizes the highly metaphysical and ambiguous nature of eschatological verses in the Qur'an. He points out that linking such verses to specific scientific models is speculative, especially given that a Big Crunch, if it occurs at all, would take place tens of billions of years from now – contrary to the Qur'anic depiction of a sudden, dramatic Day of Judgment. Thus, he cautions against reading modern cosmology into scriptural eschatology too literally (Guessoum, 2011: 191).

Given the differing interpretations of Altaie and Guessoum, one might wonder whether Qur'an 21:104 conflicts with modern cosmology. At first glance, there appears to be a tension: no contemporary cosmological model – whether it predicts a Big Crunch, heat death, or eternal expansion – includes the emergence of a new world in which resurrected beings live forever. However, this perceived conflict is more apparent than real. Physics and cosmology aim to describe the natural evolution of the universe under the assumption of no external intervention. The Qur'anic account, by contrast, refers to a divinely initiated eschatological transformation – a miraculous act that lies beyond the scope of empirical science. Therefore, one can coherently affirm both the predictive power of modern cosmology and the literal sense of the verse. Scientific models describe the cosmos up to the point of divine intervention, while the Qur'anic verse describes what happens after that intervention.

Moreover, the new creation alluded to in the verse need not be governed by the current laws of physics, since it represents an entirely different ontological order. From this perspective, even if the verse evokes imagery akin to a cosmic collapse or Big Crunch, there remains no inherent contradiction with mainstream models that predict a perpetually expanding universe.

In my opinion, these are the only verses directly related to physical cosmology, as they refer to physical substances or processes. None of them presents a compelling cosmological picture that challenges modern cosmology. Hence, there is, so far, no conflict between the Qur'an's cosmological narrative and the modern, scientific cosmological model.

Before moving on to the next topic, I would like to highlight some crucial points in the Qur'an related to physical cosmology. First, the Qur'an describes the universe as being created with purpose and balance, not as a random occurrence:

> And We did not create the heaven and earth and that between them in play. (*al-Anbiyā'* 21:16)
>
> Indeed, all things We created with measure. (*al-Qamar* 54:49)

Second, the Qur'an encourages humans to reflect upon the creation of the universe as a means to understand and appreciate the Creator. The creation serves as a sign for humans to recognize the existence and greatness of Allah:

> Indeed, in the creation of the heavens and the earth and the alternation of the night and the day are signs for those of understanding. (*al 'Imrān* 3:190)

In the following section, we will explore whether modern cosmology can verify these claims of the Qur'an. For now, we will move on to a subject that has been a topic of extensive debate in the Islamic tradition.

2.4 The Qur'an and Creation Ex Nihilo

In Islamic theology and exegesis, the dominant view is that Allah created the universe from nothing (ex nihilo). However, some Islamic philosophers in the Aristotelian tradition have argued that the universe was created from a primary material element or that it is eternal but contingent, its existence being eternally caused by God. In the next section, we will analyze different philosophical creation models in the Islamic tradition.

One of the critical issues for which Abū Ḥāmid al-Ghazālī (1058–1111) denounced the Peripatetic philosophers, such as Abū 'Alī ibn Sīnā (Avicenna) (980–1037), was their belief in the eternity of the universe (al-Ghazālī, 2000: 226). Al-Ghazālī not only employed philosophical arguments against the eternity of the universe – such as the impossibility of an actual infinite and the impossibility of traversing one – but also raised theological concerns about the aseity of God, meaning that God is entirely self-existent and that all other beings depend on Him for their existence.

Since the time of the first philosophical theologians in the Islamic tradition (the *Mu'tazilah)*, theologians have worried that belief in multiple eternal entities would undermine the principle of *Tawḥīd* which holds that there is one God (which, according to the *Mu'tazilah*, implies just one eternal entity).

The later Peripatetic philosopher Abū Walīd ibn Rushd (Averroes) (1126–1198) criticizes Al-Ghazālī's arguments against the eternity of the universe. Ibn Rushd argues that the Qur'an's verses on the creation of the universe primarily aim to illustrate that all existence is a manifestation of divine power and grace. He emphasizes that nothing in the universe originated spontaneously or by chance. The Qur'an communicates this concept to its initial audience using simple and direct language, avoiding complex philosophical discourse. Furthermore, the Qur'an often conveys essential knowledge through tangible examples relevant to everyday life, much like its depictions of the afterlife. However, on subjects not critical for religious or moral understanding, such as the nature of the soul, the Qur'an adopts a stance of "You do not need to know this," refraining from engaging in purely intellectual discussions. Put simply, Ibn Rushd thinks the Qur'an is not a scientific textbook (and so should not be read as such) (Ibn Rushd, 1998: 161–162).

As a result, Ibn Rushd cautions against interpreting the Qur'an in ways that delve into speculative matters, such as "creation from nothing" or "creation from material elements." He advises against imposing any such philosophical interpretations onto its verses. Ibn Rushd's caution is worth heeding: *imposing speculative philosophical stances on the Qur'an is just as problematic as imposing scientific theories on the Qur'an.*

According to Ibn Rushd, the creation of the universe is a unique event that cannot be directly observed and, therefore, cannot be compared with everyday observable events. He argues that conveying this concept to the general populace is feasible only through metaphors, such as "creation in six days," "His throne was upon the water," or "He directed Himself to the heaven while it was smoke." Consequently, Ibn Rushd believes that the Qur'an does not explicitly describe the universe's creation ex nihilo, since such a concept would have been incomprehensible to the masses (Ibn Rushd, 1998: 171–173). Additionally, he warns against hastily concluding that the Qur'an supports the idea of ex nihilo creation, especially since it hints at the existence of pre-universal materials like water or smoke (Ibn Rushd, 1998: 42–43).

Ibn Rushd suggests that discussions on the universe's origin should be based on philosophical reasoning rather than Qur'anic interpretation.

Again, Ibn Rushd's position on this issue does not reflect the common approach in Islamic theology, which generally favors the concept of creation ex nihilo. What scriptural arguments can be presented to support creation ex nihilo?

One commonly cited Qur'anic phrase alleged to support creation ex nihilo is *kun fa-yakūn,* which translates as "Be, and it is." This phrase appears in several verses of the Qur'an, emphasizing Allah's effortless ability to create. It is also used in reference to the creation of the universe:

> It is He who created the heavens and the earth in truth. And the day He says, "Be," and it is, His word is the truth ... (*al-An'ām* 6:73)

However, the same expression is used in the Qur'an for the creation of Jesus (Isa), who was not created ex nihilo:

> She said, "My Lord, how will I have a child when no man has touched me?" He said, "Such is Allah; He creates what He wills. When He decrees a matter, He only says to it, 'Be,' and it is." (*al-'Imrān* 3:47)

Therefore, the expression *kun fa-yakūn* does not imply creation ex nihilo in every instance.

In my view, there are just two scriptural arguments that apparently support creation ex nihilo, though neither provides indisputable proof. The first is found in the following verse:

> He to whom belongs the dominion of the heavens and the earth, who has not taken a son and has no partner in dominion; and He created everything and determined it with precise determination. (*al-Furqān* 25:2)

This verse explicitly states that Allah is the creator of "everything" (*kulla shay'in*), encompassing all that exists without exception. This is often taken to imply that God created the universe ex nihilo, since nothing can exist prior to the universe. However, this assumption is not necessarily right. It is possible that Allah created our universe from a preexisting substance, some form of matter that predates our visible universe. This interpretation would still affirm that Allah is the creator of everything, but allows for the possibility that the universe was formed from a preexisting substance created previously.

Similar verses use the term *Badī'*, usually translated as "Originator." One example is:

> He is the Originator of the heavens and the earth. How could He have a son when He does not have a companion and He created all things? And He is, of all things, Knowing. (*al-An'ām* 6:101)

Again, to infer creation ex nihilo from these verses, we must assume that nothing existed before our observable universe.

To conclude, while it is certainly possible and perhaps even probable to interpret that God created our universe ex nihilo, no verse in the Qur'an necessitates this belief. Consequently, the Qur'an is compatible with the possibility that God created our universe from some pre-existing substance.

We will revisit this question when we discuss the multiverse. For now, we move on to analyze the various philosophical cosmological models discussed within the Islamic intellectual tradition.

2.5 Philosophical Models of Creation in the Islamic Tradition

In Islamic thought, a prevailing agreement among Muslim theologians and philosophers is that God is the creator and that the cosmos is causally dependent on Him. There are at least four different models that aim to explain God's creative act. This section will analyze these four models and compare their compatibility with modern scientific cosmology.

The first model, advocated by Muslim Peripatetic philosophers, holds that the world emanates or flows from the essence of God, implying a continuous and necessary outpouring of existence from the divine. One famous defender of this model is Ibn Sīnā. Emanation posits two main ideas: the universe eternally proceeds from God, and God's causation is mediated, meaning that lower entities emerge from higher ones rather than directly from God (McGinnis & Acar, 2023).

In Ibn Sīnā's philosophy, God is the Necessary Existent (*al-wājib al-wujūd*); God must exist and cannot not exist. He is also absolutely simple, without parts or potentiality for change. Ibn Sīnā argued that the Necessary Being must be simple because it is indivisible and lacks composition; any composition would render its existence contingent on its parts, contradicting its necessary existence. Additionally, simplicity implies immutability, as a being without parts cannot change, maintaining its perfection and eternal nature.

However, if God were to create at a specific moment in time, it would imply a change in His will or essence, which contradicts divine simplicity and immutability. Since God is unchanging and exists eternally, His act of creation must also be eternal. Therefore, as the effect of God's eternal creative act, the cosmos must have always existed and will continue to exist perpetually. Any temporal beginning of creation would suggest a before and after in God's will, introducing change into God's nature and compromising His simplicity.

Ibn Sīnā differentiates God's knowledge from human knowledge. While humans acquire knowledge through interaction with the world, God, being free of potentiality and absolutely simple, is completely independent of external sources. Instead, God knows Himself perfectly as the ultimate cause of all existence. And, in knowing Himself, God inherently and completely knows the cosmos as His effect. God's self-knowledge causes the cosmos to exist, leading to the conclusion that the universe eternally emanates from God's self-knowledge (Ibn Sina, 2005: 288–298).

Ibn Sīnā considers it almost heretical to claim that God began to create at a specific moment, as this would imply a change in God's will and contradict divine simplicity and the doctrine of *Tawḥīd*. Regarding God's will, he argues that while God's act of creation is a free act of will, it does not involve intention or choice among options. Such processes would imply deliberation and composition, which are incompatible with God's simplicity. God acts freely because He knows and consents to His action without being forced, but His action does not involve selecting among alternatives.

The second model, favored by *Kalām* theologians, is that of temporal origination, where the universe is brought into existence at a specific point in time (McGinnis & Acar, 2023). This view is often combined with occasionalism, the belief that God is the sole active agent of all events. Al-Ghazālī, a well-known advocate of temporal origination, argued against the idea of an eternal universe by claiming that an endless sequence of past events is logically incoherent (Al-Ghazālī, 2013: 27–41). He reasoned that if the universe were to lack a beginning, it would require moving through an infinite series of prior events to get to the present, which he believed is nonsensical.

Theologians also criticized Ibn Sīnā's interpretation of voluntary action. They argued that emanation is a natural, involuntary process – like the sun shining without choice. Since, they argued, a genuinely free act must involve choice, any action lacking choice is not free. al-Ghazālī attacked the argument from divine simplicity outlined earlier, claiming that divine simplicity conflicted with belief in distinct divine attributes such as life, power, knowledge, and will (McGinnis, 2022).

A significant challenge for the theologian who affirms immutability is explaining how a change in God's will – from willing not to create to willing to create – can occur without a change in God Himself. If God is the ultimate cause, nothing external can prompt this change. al-Ghazālī proposes that God eternally willed to create the world at the specific moment it began (al-Ghazālī, 2000: 12–46). Thus, God wills the creation of the world without any change in the divine will.

However, this solution faces criticism because it raises the question of why God chose that specific moment of creation over any other. Given that an infinite number of moments are equally possible, either there must be a reason for God's specific choice (which implies outside causation) or the choice is arbitrary and irrational. Neither option is satisfactory to the theologian.

Ghazālī responds by redefining the essential function of the will. He asserts that the will's primary role is to choose among indistinguishable options without any external cause influencing the particular choice made. This choice – the selection among indistinguishable options – is not arbitrary in the sense of being random or baseless but is purely an act of will. He uses the example of a starving man selecting one piece of identical food items without any specific reason for choosing that particular piece (al-Ghazālī, 2000: 23–24). The man acts rationally by choosing and eating rather than starving due to indecision. Applying this to God, Ghazālī argues that God, from eternity, wills to create without any change in His will, and the specific moment of creation is determined solely by His will without external causation. This maintains God's immutability and affirms that His action is the rational act of a volitional agent.

The third model presents creation as a manifestation of a single ultimate reality. This perspective is mainly upheld by Sufis and mystically inclined thinkers who emphasize the immanence of God in all aspects of the universe. They view the material world as a reflection or expression of the divine reality. The most sophisticated defenders of this model are Muḥyī al-Dīn ibn ʿArabī (1165–1240) and Mullā Ṣadrā (1571–1640). We will cover Mullā Ṣadrā's theory here (Ṣadrā, 2014: 68–71). His account is based on two complex concepts: the modulation of existence (*tashkīk al-wujūd*) and substantial motion (*al-ḥaraka l-jawhariyya*).

Let's first consider the modulation of existence. Ṣadrā held that existence is the fundamental reality, with essences being secondary and derivative. He argued that all beings are manifestations of a single, dynamic reality – existence itself – which varies in intensity and gradation. This perspective emphasizes that existence precedes essence, meaning that entities first exist and then acquire their specific natures or essences. Ṣadrā holds that God represents existence at its most perfect, eternal, and unchanging limit. Only God is infinite and unchanging. Creation, however, is a manifestation of existence at varying degrees that fall short of divine perfection. This means that compared to God, all created things exhibit existence to lesser extents.

The doctrine of substantial motion asserts that change occurs not only in the accidents or attributes of substances but also within their essence. He proposed that all created beings are in a constant state of flux and transformation at the level of their substance. In other words, Ṣadrā believes that no created thing persists unchanged through time – there are no enduring matter, forms, species, or essences. Everything except God is in a constant state of evolution, not randomly, but progressively becoming more godlike as part of an unceasing journey toward divine perfection.

These two doctrines combine into a unique model of creation. Since all substances and essences are in perpetual flux, only God is eternal; everything else comes into existence after not having existed. This aligns him with theologians who view creation as a temporal event – things coming to be after nonexistence.

Ṣadrā's concept of substantial motion resonates with emanationist thought. He allows that, infinitely into the past and future, God is the continuous source of existence, constantly creating as creation evolves. While God's creative act is eternal, nothing in the created order remains the same long enough to have always existed. This process reflects the gradational nature of existence, where all entities are interconnected and in a state of perpetual motion toward greater existential intensity. Ṣadrā's theory reconciles the philosophical notion of an eternal universe with the theological concept of a created one. By emphasizing the continuous and dynamic nature of creation, he bridges the gap between the temporal beginning of the universe and its eternal dependence on the Divine.

The fourth model, introduced by the traditionalist and literalist Ibn Taymiyyah (1263–1328), who later inspired Salafī interpretations, posits a perpetually creating God (Hoover, 2004). Ibn Taymiyyah presents a theological view where God's perfection is characterized by perpetual dynamism rather than timeless eternity, setting him apart from *Kalām* theology and Peripatetic philosophy. Adopting an Aristotelian perspective on time, he holds that while God neither exists within time nor transcends it, time originates from God's internal dynamism and His continuous act of creation (Ibn Taymiyyah, 1995: vol. 18, 210–212; Ibn Taymiyyah, 1991: vol. 8, 44–46). Since God has been performing successive actions for eternity, time has always existed, but time does not have an independent existence apart from God's movements. Ibn Taymiyyah prefers to discuss this dynamism in terms of God's voluntary attributes (*al-ṣifāt al-ikhtiyāriyya*), which include creation, love, mercy, wrath, and justice. These attributes reside within God's essence and are exercised through His will and power (Ibn Taymiyyah, 1995: vol. 8, 471).

According to Ibn Taymiyyah, creation is voluntary. However, he argues that God's perfection entails that He has always willed to create, exercising His power from eternity without a beginning (*min al-azal*) (Ibn Taymiyyah, 1995: vol. 18, 202–203, 235). While each created thing has a beginning, and none is eternal alongside God, Ibn Taymiyyah holds that God has eternally willed to create, such that there has always been some created entity in existence. The current world was formed from prior materials previously created by God, extending infinitely into the past (Ibn Taymiyyah, 1991: vol. 8, 54–55). Ibn Taymiyyah refers to the "genus" or "species" of created things as eternal in this sense but denies that this genus exists independently in reality. In an endless history of creation, only created things with beginnings exist extra-mentally.

Ibn Taymiyyah's view aligns more closely with peripatetic philosophers like Ibn Sīnā and Ibn Rushd than with *Kalām* theologians. He concurs that God's perfection results in the world's existence but rejects Ibn Sīnā's emanation theory in favor of God's continuous creation. He also adopts the peripatetic philosophers' critique of the *Kalām* concept of creation ex nihilo. If the world had a beginning, God would have been imperfect before creating and subject to change upon initiating creation. An efficient cause would have been required to trigger God's action. While *Kalām* theologians argue that God's will inherently begins the world's origination without needing an external cause, Ibn Taymiyyah dismisses this as an impossibility, labeling it *tarjīḥ bilā murajjiḥ* ("preponderance without a preponderant cause") (Ibn Taymiyyah, 1991: vol. 8, 140).

In this section, we have analyzed four competing philosophical models of creation. All four models were devised by thinkers well versed in both the Qur'an and Islamic sciences, and they explicitly used Qur'anic verses to defend their respective models. I believe there are two key lessons to be learned from this analysis.

First, scripture is open to various interpretations. This is unsurprising, as the Qur'an's primary aim was not to provide a philosophical or scientific cosmological model of the universe. An analogy with the concept of underdetermination of theory by data (Stanford, 2023) in the philosophy of science may be useful here. Underdetermination refers to the idea that a given body of empirical evidence can support multiple, mutually incompatible scientific theories. This occurs because the data available at any given time may be insufficient to decisively confirm or refute competing theories. In other words, empirical data alone cannot determine which theory is true.

By analogy, different theological interpretations or philosophical models that attempt to explain and systematize the teachings of the Qur'an are like scientific theories. Theological models aim to provide coherent and comprehensive accounts of what the scripture means and how it relates to broader questions about God, creation, and metaphysics. Just as in science, the "data" (scripture) underdetermine the correct interpretation. Multiple, often competing, theological models can explain and accommodate the same scriptural data.

Second, when we move to scientific models, another layer of underdetermination emerges. Any theological or philosophical model can be adjusted to align with scientific accounts. To illustrate this, let us compare the four models discussed here with the modern scientific perspective.

The temporal origination model is typically considered compatible with modern cosmology, as the observable universe appears to have begun to exist according to the standard inflationary model. However, if the chaotic inflation model is correct, and our universe is one among many "bubble universes" that did not emerge ex nihilo, the temporal origination model remains viable. Defenders of the temporal origination model could argue that by "universe," they mean the entire multiverse, which originated in time. The only challenging case would be an eternal multiverse. However, proving that the multiverse is eternal may not be possible. Even if we develop a successful, empirically sound cosmological model with an eternal past, proponents of the temporal origination model could accept it as a description of the universe's current and far-past state while denying that it proves the universe is eternal. They would insist that creation is a miraculous event where natural laws break down, claiming there was a specific moment in the far past when the universe began to exist, evolving under the laws described by the cosmological model since that moment.

The perpetually creating God model and the creation as manifestation model naturally align with multiverse theories such as chaotic inflation. However, even if multiverse theories were proven false and there was nothing before the Big Bang, the perpetually creating God model and the creation as manifestation model would not be falsified. Defenders of these models could argue that other universes, whether manifested or created, are entirely separate from our own and inaccessible through our physical sciences. If we were to discover that our universe itself is eternal and the Big Bang model is false – though this is extremely unlikely – these models could still accommodate an eternal universe; they could claim that temporal continuity in the universe is an illusion and that the universe persists only because God continuously manifests or recreates it. Because each successive creation appears to pick up where the last left off, the illusion of an eternal universe persists. Thus, while science may favor a model of a single eternal universe, such a model is consistent, in some broadly logical sense, with each of these philosophical frameworks.

While the emanation model aligns most naturally with an eternal universe, with certain metaphysical adjustments, it can be reconciled with a finite universe. For example, one could posit other universes physically separated from ours and reinterpret Ibn Sīnā's concept of the universe as a multiverse encompassing these separate entities.

Since the Qur'an, I've argued, does not force us to accept a single philosophical model and each of the most prominent models can be made to accommodate a wider variety of scientific views, there is no conflict between Qur'anic cosmology and scientific cosmology. As argued, the underdetermination of theology by the Qur'anic data mitigates against a definitive "Qur'anic cosmology." Many and varied Qur'anic cosmologies are possible; none is necessary, and all are revisable. Religious cosmologies and the theological or philosophical models derived from them can always be refined to align with scientific findings. Given that observation is considered a valid source of knowledge in

Islamic theology, refining religious models in light of scientific discoveries could even be viewed as a religious duty. This approach is not "inventing" religion but striving to discover the correct interpretation of religious cosmology through careful analysis of both God's revelation and God's world.

3 Divine Precision: Fine-Tuning and Islamic Theology

Teleological or design arguments aim to demonstrate the existence of God as a designer based on specific features of the universe that exhibit purpose or order. While the two terms are often used interchangeably, *teleological arguments* appeal more broadly to apparent purpose or goal-directedness in nature, whereas *design arguments* typically involve analogies to human-made artifacts and infer a designer from the complexity or functionality (design) of natural phenomena. Teleological arguments are one of the oldest forms of argument for the existence of God and have been defended by thinkers such as Plato, the Stoics, al-Ghazālī, Ibn Rushd, Thomas Aquinas, Isaac Newton, and Gottfried Wilhelm Leibniz. It has also been critiqued by figures like Lucretius, David Hume, Immanuel Kant, and Søren Kierkegaard.[14]

While Muslim theologians have traditionally preferred cosmological arguments to defend the existence of God, teleological arguments have also held a significant and recurring place in Islamic thought. al-Ghazālī, for example, devotes an entire treatise to contemplating divine wisdom in the natural world (al-Ghazālī, 1993), emphasizing how the structure of creation points to a purposeful Creator. Similarly, Fakhr al-Dīn al-Rāzī frequently invokes teleological reasoning in his Qur'anic exegesis, highlighting the harmony and suitability of the cosmos as signs of divine intent.

Ibn Rushd, who criticized the cosmological arguments advanced by Ibn Sīnā and the theologians, proposed instead what he considered the Qur'an's argument for the existence of God: teleological arguments. He defended two forms of the argument.

The first, known as the *Argument from Providence* (*Dalīl al-'Ināyah*), focuses on the order and apparent intentionality in the universe (Ibn Rushd, 1998, 24–28). Ibn Rushd points to the intricate interdependence of natural phenomena – such as the cycles of day and night, celestial movements, and the Earth's suitability for life – as evidence of the Creator's deliberate design. Aligning his reasoning with Qur'anic verses, he urges contemplation of the cosmos as a means of recognizing God. Although the argument might seem anthropocentric, Ibn Rushd stresses that divine providence encompasses and values the

---

[14] For a comprehensive overview of the history of teleological argument as well as its different forms, see (Jantzen, 2014).

entire universe. While Ibn Rushd presents the Argument from Providence as compelling, later philosophers such as David Hume challenged whether apparent order implies intentional design.

The second argument, the *Argument from Creation* (*Dalīl al-Ikhtirā'*), highlights the transformation of inanimate matter into animate beings and the intricate interdependence observed in creation (Ibn Rushd, 1998, 24–28). While Ibn Rushd's Argument from Creation reflects the scientific understanding of his time, it differs from modern abiogenesis, which affirms the gradual emergence of life from nonliving matter through complex chemical processes.

Ibn Rushd's observation that the Qur'an's primary argument for the existence of God is teleological is insightful. Hundreds of verses in the Qur'an urge readers to reflect on the design and providence evident in natural phenomena. Some examples include:

- He who created the seven heavens in layers. You do not see in the creation of the Most Merciful any inconsistency. So return your vision to the sky, do you see any breaks? (*al-Mulk*, 67:3)
- And He created everything and determined it with precise measure. (*al-Furqān*, 25:2)
- Do they not look at the camels – how they are created? And at the sky – how it is raised? And at the mountains – how they are erected? And at the earth – how it is spread out? (*al-Ghāshiyah*, 88:17–20)

In this section, we will analyze how contemporary cosmology can support a form of teleological argument resembling Ibn Rushd's Argument from Providence and affirm the Qur'an's claim that the universe is determined with precise order.[15]

3.1 The Fine-Tuning of the Universe for Life

A universe capable of sustaining life is one that could support beings that can reproduce, store, and use energy, that is, have metabolism. Such conditions can only be provided by a universe exhibiting stable energy sources and a rich chemistry capable of yielding molecular structures, reproduction, and energy storage.

In the 1970s – following classic papers by Brandon Carter (Carter, 1974), Bernard Carr, and Martin Rees (Carr & Rees, 1979), as well as the work of Paul Davies (Davies, 1983) and the extensive study by John Barrow and Frank Tipler (Barrow & Tipler, 1986) – physicists realized that the set of possible laws, constants, and initial conditions of the universe conducive to the emergence of

---

[15] Part of the material discussed here has been published in (Doko, 2019a) and (Doko, 2019b).

stable energy sources (e.g., stars), as well as chemistry (and, therefore, life), is extremely small. This realization was termed the "fine-tuning" of the universe for life. Since the 1970s, examples of fine-tuning have increased extensively,[16] and physicists and philosophers have sought to account for – or questioned whether there is a need to account for – fine-tuning.

Examples of fine-tuning can be categorized into three groups:

1. The fine-tuning of the laws of nature.
2. The fine-tuning of the fundamental physical constants.
3. The fine-tuning of the initial conditions of the universe.

In the next subsections, we will provide several examples from each category.

3.1.1 The Fine-Tuning of the Laws of Nature

The first category of examples of fine-tuning pertains to the laws of nature. If the fundamental laws governing the universe were different, life could not have developed. To illustrate, let us consider the four fundamental forces:

Gravity

Gravity is a long-range attractive force between material objects. In classical mechanics, this force is mathematically expressed as $F = GmM/r^2$, where F denotes the gravitational force, M and m represent the masses of two objects, r is the distance between them, and G is the universal gravitational constant. If gravity did not exist, or if it were repulsive or a short-range force (like the strong nuclear force), the formation of stars and planets would have been impossible. Stars, which primarily form from hydrogen and helium atoms, rely on gravitational attraction to coalesce. Without stars, the synthesis of elements heavier than hydrogen, helium, and lithium – which occurs in stellar cores – would not have occurred. Since life depends on complex elements and stable energy sources (i.e., stars), the absence or alteration of gravity would preclude the possibility of life in our universe.

Electrostatic Force

The electrostatic force is a long-range force that acts between charged objects. It is attractive for opposite charges and repulsive for like charges. Mathematically, it is described by $F = kqQ/r^2$, where F denotes the electrostatic force, q and Q are the charge magnitudes, k is a constant determining the strength of the force, and r

---

[16] For technical reviews of the progress in the field, the reader may consult (Hogan, 2000) and (Barnes, 2012). For popular level presentations see (Rees, 1999) and (Davies, 2007).

is the distance between the charges. This force holds negatively charged electrons in orbit around positively charged nuclei, enabling the formation of atoms. If the electrostatic force did not exist, or if its behavior were reversed (attractive for like charges and repulsive for opposites), atoms would not form, preventing the existence of chemistry, stable energy sources, and, ultimately, life.

Strong Nuclear Force

The strong nuclear force is a short-range force that binds positively charged protons and neutral neutrons together in atomic nuclei. Without the strong nuclear force, or if it were repulsive or weaker than the electromagnetic force, only hydrogen nuclei would exist, as no other atomic nuclei could form. Conversely, if the strong nuclear force were long-range (like gravity or electromagnetic force), atoms would fail to form, resulting in large, uniform structures rather than distinct atomic nuclei. In either case, life would be impossible.

Weak Nuclear Force

The weak nuclear force governs radioactive decay and plays a crucial role in stellar processes and the creation of elements. Without this force, the formation of complex elements in stars would not occur, and the energy required to power stars would be absent. Consequently, biological molecules and life could not arise.

The fine-tuning of the laws of nature extends beyond these four fundamental forces. For instance, if electrons were bosons rather than fermions, they would condense into the lowest energy state, rendering complex chemistry impossible. Similarly, if subatomic phenomena were governed by classical mechanics rather than quantum mechanics, stable atoms could not form – an electron would radiate all of its kinetic energy and spiral into its nucleus.

3.1.2 The Fine-Tuning of the Fundamental Physical Constants

In addition to the laws of nature, fundamental physical constants must also fall within a narrow range of values. For example, if G, the gravitational constant, had a larger value, masses would attract each other with a stronger force than is actually the case. Indeed, such constants allow for the emergence of life only within particularly narrow ranges. As Stephen Hawking and Leonard Mlodinow put it:

> Most of the fundamental constants in our theories appear fine-tuned in the sense that if they were altered by only modest amounts, the universe would be qualitatively different, and in many cases unsuitable for the development of life ... The emergence of the complex structures capable of supporting intelligent observers seems to be very fragile. The laws of nature form a system that is extremely fine-tuned, and very little in physical law can be

altered without destroying the possibility of the development of life as we know it. Were it not for a series of startling coincidences in the precise details of physical law, it seems, humans and similar life-forms would never have come into being. (Hawking & Mlodinow, 2010)

Let us consider some examples of the fine-tuning of fundamental physical constants:

The Strength of Gravity (α_G)

Gravity is approximately 10^{40} times weaker than the strong nuclear force, making it extraordinarily weak compared to the other three fundamental forces. This means that, for example, the gravitational attraction between two protons is vastly weaker than the strong nuclear force that binds them together inside an atomic nucleus. To put this in perspective, the difference in strength is far greater than the weight of the Earth compared to a grain of sand – about ten billion times stronger. If the strength of gravity were increased such that it was no longer weaker than the strong nuclear force by a factor of approximately 10^{37}, stars like our Sun would burn out too quickly to support life. This would render the emergence of life extremely improbable (Collins, 2003).[17] Another striking example of fine-tuning can be observed by comparing gravity's strength to factors determining the expansion rate of the Big Bang, such as the density of mass-energy in the early universe. If the strength of gravity had been weaker or stronger by one part in 10^{60}, ceteris paribus (i.e., all other things being equal), the universe would have either expanded too rapidly for stars to form or collapsed too quickly for life to emerge (Davies, 1982: 89).

The Cosmological Constant (Λ)

This term, which Einstein introduced in his equations of general relativity, regulates the expansion rate of the universe. If Λ is positive, it acts as a repulsive force, causing the expansion of space; if negative, it acts as an attractive force, contracting space. Predictions from quantum field theory suggest that the cosmological constant should be 10^{120} times greater than the observed value – undoubtedly the greatest estimation error in physics. This discrepancy implies the existence of a cancellation mechanism that matches the quantum vacuum term to at least 120 decimal places. As Steven Weinberg explained:

> There may be a cosmological constant in the field equations whose value just cancels the effects of the vacuum mass density produced by quantum fluctuations. However, to avoid conflict with astronomical observation, this

---

[17] We assume the strength of the strong nuclear force as the maximum possible value of strength of gravity.

cancellation would have to be accurate to at least 120 decimal places. Why in the world should the cosmological constant be so precisely fine-tuned? (Weinberg, 1977: 186–187)

If this cancellation mechanism were off by even one decimal place, it would preclude life (Davies, 2007: 166–170). For instance, a slight increase in the cosmological constant would inhibit the formation of galaxies and stars (Weinberg, 1987). Conversely, if it were smaller, the universe would have collapsed before life could emerge.

The Dimensionality of the Universe (D)

Our universe has three spatial dimensions and one temporal dimension, the only combination capable of sustaining life. If there were an additional temporal dimension, no massive particles would be stable (Dorling, 1970), making chemistry impossible. Similarly, a deviation in the number of spatial dimensions would lead to the instability of atoms and planets (Ehrenfest, 1917), rendering life impossible.[18]

3.1.3 The Fine-Tuning of the Initial Conditions of the Universe

The fate of the universe is determined not only by the laws of nature and the fundamental constants but also by its initial conditions. Remarkably, these initial conditions also appear to be fine-tuned. Consider two prominent examples:

The Amplitude of Primordial Fluctuations (Q)

This parameter represents the energy required to break up and disperse the largest structures, such as galactic clusters, expressed as a fraction of the rest mass energy of that structure. It is a dimensionless constant with a value of approximately $Q \approx 10^{-5}$. If Q were smaller than 10^{-6}, gas would never condense into gravitationally bound structures, thereby preventing the formation of stars. Conversely, if Q were greater than 10^{-5}, the universe would have been excessively turbulent and violent: structures larger than galaxies would have formed in the early universe, but instead of fragmenting into stars, they would collapse into giant black holes with masses exceeding those of galaxy clusters (Rees, 1999: 115). In either case, life as we know it would be impossible.[19]

---

[18] For more a careful analysis of the fine-tuning of the dimensionality of space-time, the reader may want to consult (Tegmark, 1997).

[19] For a more technical and careful analysis of the fine-tuning of the amplitude of primordial fluctuations, see (Tegmark & Rees, 1998) and (Tegmark et al., 2006).

The Initial Entropy of the Universe (S)

Entropy measures the disorder in a system, and as a system becomes more disordered, its entropy increases. The Second Law of Thermodynamics states that the entropy of the universe increases over time. However, the initial entropy of our universe was extraordinarily low (Davies, 1984: 168), which allowed the development of ordered structures over billions of years. If the initial entropy had been higher, the resultant disorder would have prohibited the emergence of life. Theoretical physicist Roger Penrose calculated that the number of possible initial states of the universe is on the order of $10^{10^{123}}$. Among these states, only one resembles our universe, meaning the probability of our universe's initial state arising by chance is approximately $1/10^{10^{123}}$ (Penrose, 1989: 339–345; Penrose, 2004: 728). This is an example of incredibly precise fine-tuning – the number of possible initial states far exceeds the total number of particles (baryons, electrons, photons, etc.) in the universe, which is estimated to be on the order of 10^{90}.

3.2 Fine-Tuning as an Evidence for Theism

The examples of fine-tuning outlined earlier raise the question of whether they require explanation and, if so, what that explanation might be. If fine-tuning requires an explanation and if theism provides a superior explanation to its alternatives, we will have a strong argument in favor of theism. The argument can be summarized as follows:

1. The fine-tuning of the universe requires explanation.
2. There is a theistic explanation: that God designed the universe for the emergence of life.
3. There is no comparably satisfying nontheistic explanation of why the universe is fine-tuned.
4. Therefore, the fine-tuning of the universe provides evidential support for theism.

This argument follows the "inference to the best explanation" approach. Much of our scientific and everyday beliefs rely on this kind of inference. For instance, although we have never directly observed electrons, we strongly believe in their existence because positing electrons provides the best explanation of many phenomena (compared to explanations that do not posit their existence).

The first premise is compelling. Given that an extremely small subset of possible configurations of physical laws, constants, and initial conditions permits life, our universe's membership in that subset is highly surprising. Nearly all physicists and philosophers familiar with the fine-tuning of the universe agree that this surprising fact demands some kind of explanation. The apparent need for explanation arises from the magnitude of the improbabilities involved.

For example, as noted earlier, the cosmological constant must be set to a precision of 1 in 10^{120}. To grasp how small this probability is, consider that there are approximately 100 million atoms in one centimeter, each composed of electrons, protons, and neutrons. The observable universe contains more than 100 billion galaxies, each with billions of stars, and the total number of particles in the universe is roughly 10^{90}. The probability of randomly selecting one specific particle from all the particles in the universe is still billions of times higher than the improbability of 1 in 10^{120}.

Choosing one hidden grain of sand randomly in a desert seems impossible, but it is still far more likely than the precision required for the cosmological constant. This is just one example among many fine-tuned parameters and laws. If the probabilities were more moderate, say 1 in 10, we might reasonably dismiss the need for an explanation. However, probabilities as extreme as 1 in 10^{120} are too significant to ignore. Next, we will analyze objections that claim fine-tuning does not require explanation.

The second premise also seems intuitive. According to the theistic account, the universe was created by an omnipotent and omniscient God with the intention of creating life. Given God's desire, knowledge, and power, it would be unsurprising that the universe possesses all the necessary conditions for life. Every day experience supports the idea that low-probability outcomes suggest intention, knowledge, and power.

For example, consider a safe with an extremely complex cipher, which is highly unlikely to be opened by chance. If someone were to succeed in opening it, the most natural explanation would be that they intentionally and knowingly entered the correct cipher. Similarly, the fine-tuning of the universe can be interpreted as indicative of a purposeful and powerful agent.

The third premise asserts that nontheistic explanations are less compelling than the theistic explanation. To assess this claim, we must analyze the primary nontheistic alternatives: more fundamental law and multiverse. We will analyze these alternatives next.

If the three premises outlined earlier hold, then the argument for theism based on fine-tuning is a powerful one. In the next sections, we will evaluate objections to the argument and assess nontheistic explanations for fine-tuning.

3.3 Objections to the First Premise: Fine-Tuning Does Not Require Explanation

Some philosophers and scientists deny the claim that fine-tuning requires explanation. They either deny that the universe is fine-tuned for existence or else think that we should not be surprised that the universe is fine-tuned, and therefore should not search for an explanation. Let us consider each of these claims.

3.3.1 Statistics

One response to fine-tuning is to deny the need for explanation, arguing that every possible universe is equally unlikely. This view likens fine-tuning to a lottery: suppose Kaan wins a lottery with ten million participants. While his win is highly improbable, it requires no special explanation because every participant had the same low chance of winning (and one person must win). Similarly, the fine-tuning of the universe could be seen as the result of a cosmic lottery, explainable by pure chance.

This analogy fails for two reasons. First, in a lottery, all outcomes are equivalent in value – no particular winner is inherently special. The event of someone winning is expected, even if the specific winner is surprising. By contrast, a life-permitting universe is vastly different from other possible outcomes, as the majority of configurations would not allow life. Life-permitting universes are an exceedingly rare subset, making their occurrence improbable and surprising.

Second, the improbability of fine-tuning is far greater than that of a typical lottery. Fine-tuning involves constants requiring precision as extreme as 1 in 10^{60} or 10^{120}. Such astronomical improbability cannot reasonably be attributed to pure chance, suggesting the need for a more robust explanation.

3.3.2 The Weak Anthropic Principle

Some thinkers appeal to the Weak Anthropic Principle (WAP) to respond to the demand for an explanation of fine-tuning (Carter, 1974). The WAP holds that if the physical laws and constants were not compatible with life, we would not exist to observe them. Hence, our observation of a life-permitting universe is unsurprising – we could not have observed otherwise.

While WAP itself is a descriptive constraint on observation, it is sometimes invoked as a way of dismissing the need for deeper explanation of fine-tuning. However, WAP also plays a more constructive role in physics, where it is used to constrain theoretical models by ensuring that their parameter ranges allow for the emergence of complexity, life, or intelligence. In this sense, it serves as a heuristic in evaluating which physical theories are compatible with the existence of observers like us.

This reasoning, however, is widely criticized as fallacious. It is akin to saying that a person who survives jumping from the fiftieth floor should not be surprised because, had they not survived, they would not be here to question it. Clearly, such an extraordinary event demands an explanation, regardless of the survivor's ability to observe it. Similarly, the surprising aspect of fine-tuning is not merely that we observe it, it represents an extraordinarily improbable outcome requiring explanation.

3.3.3 Other Forms of Life Are Possible

A common objection to the fine-tuning argument is that it assumes that only familiar life forms are possible, ignoring the potential for exotic life in universes we consider inhospitable.

This objection misunderstands the argument. Fine-tuning does not assume life must resemble familiar forms but instead posits minimal requirements for any life: the ability to reproduce, store, and use energy. These basic conditions necessitate chemical elements for forming molecules and stable energy sources. Thus, the argument only assumes that life requires universes capable of supporting these minimal conditions. If the objector finds even these requirements too restrictive, they bear the burden of explaining how life could arise without them.

3.3.4 The Changing Single Variable Objection

Victor Stenger argues that fine-tuning analyses are flawed because they vary one parameter while holding others constant:

> ... the examples of fine-tuning given in the theist literature ... vary one parameter while holding all the rest constant. This is both dubious and scientifically shoddy. As we shall see in several specific cases, changing one or more other parameters can often compensate for the one that is changed. (Stenger, 2011: 70)

Stenger's objection is flawed for two reasons. First, even if fine-tuning calculations were based solely on varying single parameters, it would not invalidate the hypothesis. Considering multiple parameters typically reveals an even larger space of life-prohibiting universes. Second, Stenger's claim is factually incorrect. Most fine-tuning studies vary multiple parameters simultaneously. For instance, Tegmark, Aguirre, Rees, and Wilczek examine a seven-parameter phase space in their analysis (Tegmark et al., 2006).[20]

3.3.5 Normalizability Objection

Lydia McGrew, Timothy McGrew, and Eric Vestrup argue that the probabilities invoked in fine-tuning arguments are formally incoherent because they cannot

---

[20] For a more detailed and complete critique of Stenger's work, the reader may consult (Barnes, 2012).

be normalized (McGrew et al., 2001). This objection centers on the claim that assigning equal probability across an infinite range of possible values for physical constants – such as the gravitational constant – leads to either infinite total probability or zero, rendering the argument mathematically meaningless.

However, this challenge is not insurmountable. Many physical constants are not unbounded; dimensionful constants are often constrained by theoretical limits like the Planck scale, while dimensionless constants can be described using probability distributions that favor values near unity (Barnes, 2018). Moreover, fine-tuning arguments often rely on likelihoods or comparative ratios, rather than absolute probabilities, and need not conform to the strict axioms of Kolmogorovian probability (i.e., the standard probability theory formalized by Andrey Kolmogorov). These likelihoods can still support rational inferences about design versus chance, even without strict normalization.

3.4 Objections to the Second Premise

Some philosophers have denied the claim that theism can explain the fine-tuning of the universe. They either claim that theistic explanation of the fine-tuning is a form of "God of the gaps argument" or they claim that the design hypothesis is not adequate because it does not solve the problem of fine-tuning, but merely transfers it to the level of designer itself. Let us assess these objections.

3.4.1 God of the Gaps

Some philosophers argue that the fine-tuning argument is a "God of the gaps" argument, inferring God's existence from gaps in scientific knowledge (Stenger, 2004). In this view, the argument resembles claims like "Zeus causes lightning" or "God moves the planets" – attributing divine action wherever science lacks a current explanation. Since such explanations have historically been proven wrong by various scientific advances, critics suggest rejecting the fine-tuning argument on similar grounds.

This characterization misconstrues the structure of the fine-tuning argument. It does not rely on ignorance or merely highlight a gap in scientific understanding. Rather, it begins with well-established results in physics: namely, that the emergence of life requires a narrow range of physical parameters. The issue is not how these laws operate, but why they are precisely structured as they are. The fine-tuning argument considers various explanations – such as chance, physical necessity, or design – and argues that design offers the best explanation for why the universe's parameters fall within this life-permitting range.

While it is possible that future physics will uncover deeper laws constraining these constants, this would not eliminate fine-tuning; rather, the explanatory burden would shift to why such a deeper law holds. Thus, the argument is not based on filling a temporary explanatory gap, but on assessing the comparative plausibility of competing hypotheses in light of the evidence we currently possess.

3.4.2 The "Who Designed God?" Objection

Richard Dawkins popularized the "Who designed God?" objection to design arguments, asserting:

> The whole argument turns on the familiar question "who made God?" which most thinking people discover for themselves. A designer God cannot be used to explain organized complexity because any God capable of designing anything would have to be complex enough to demand the same kind of explanation in his own right. (Dawkins, 2008: 109)

A similar objection can be found in/by J.J.C. Smart:

> If we postulate God in addition to the created universe we increase the complexity of our hypothesis. We have all the complexity of the universe itself, and we have in addition the at least equal complexity of God. (The designer of an artifact must be at least as complex as the designed artifact.) (Smart, 1985)

This objection claims that invoking a designer shifts the problem of fine-tuning to the designer, who must also require explanation. Thus, the design hypothesis is said to fail.

However, this objection is a red herring. The nature of the designer is irrelevant to the fine-tuning argument. For instance, if evidence suggests that a disease is caused by a new virus, we conclude the virus exists even if we know nothing about its nature. Similarly, if fine-tuning is best explained by a designer, we can reasonably conclude that a designer exists, regardless of whether the designer requires explanation.

Additionally, the objection assumes without justification that a designer must be as complex as the artifact designed (and so requires an explanation). This assumption is questionable, especially when applied to a nonphysical designer. For example, traditional theism conceives of God as timeless, nonspatial, and lacking physical parts – attributes that render the notion of "complexity" inapplicable in the usual physical sense. Furthermore, there is no evident principle requiring that the cause of complexity must itself be complex in a similar way. Without a compelling reason to posit an additional designer for

God, one may tentatively apply Ockham's Razor as a heuristic to avoid multiplying explanatory entities beyond necessity.

Finally, even if one were to grant that God is, in some meaningful sense, more complex than the universe, it would not automatically follow that He would require a designer. The inference from complexity to design is not straightforward, and the objection would need to establish why this connection should hold universally. For instance, humans are highly complex beings, yet we do not typically regard them as "designed" in the same sense that artifacts are. This suggests that complexity, by itself, is insufficient to warrant a design inference – and more so when applied to a nonphysical, theological entity.

3.5 Objections to the Third Premise

There are two alternative explanations often offered as rivals to the theistic explanation: the postulation of a more fundamental underlying law and the multiverse hypothesis.

3.5.1 The Appeal to a More Fundamental Law

It has been suggested that, although we currently lack an explanation for the fine-tuning of the universe, future discoveries could reveal a more fundamental law that entails the current physical laws and fundamental constants. For example, theories such as String Theory[21] or Supersymmetry, though lacking evidence now, might eventually resolve the fine-tuning problem. If so, the apparent fine-tuning of our universe would no longer seem surprising.

This response faces several important limitations.

First, while it is entirely reasonable to pursue deeper physical theories as possible resolutions to the fine-tuning problem, it is important to recognize that String Theory and Supersymmetry are highly speculative at present. As such, they cannot function as established explanatory alternatives. Besides, the argument presented here does not offer a theistic explanation as a scientific theory.[22] Rather, it is proposed as a philosophical interpretation of the data. Dismissing such an interpretation solely on the grounds that it is nonnaturalistic risks begging the question against theism, especially when theistic explanations are considered within a broader metaphysical, not scientific, context.

Second, it is also possible that future discoveries in physics may reveal that the universe is even more fine-tuned for life than currently known. While it is true that deeper physical theories may ultimately explain some instances of apparent fine-tuning, it is equally true that the historical trajectory of physics has

---

[21] Given that currently String theory predicts 10^{500} different universes, this seems very unlikely.

[22] For an argument that theism is not a scientific hypothesis or theory, see (Clark, 2014).

revealed more such cases rather than fewer. Over the past several decades, the number of recognized fine-tuning parameters has grown steadily. This trend gives rise to an inductive (or meta-inductive) expectation: unless we have strong reasons to think otherwise, we may reasonably anticipate that further physical discoveries will continue to uncover additional examples of fine-tuning, rather than eliminate them. Of course, this is a tentative projection, not a certainty – but it serves to counterbalance the assumption that future science will explain fine-tuning away.

Third, if we take the objection seriously, we would have to conclude that no scientific result can ever justify any inference, since future discoveries might overturn it. This line of reasoning undermines scientific realism and leads to a form of scientific anti-realism, which is not a desirable position for most defenders of this view.[23]

Even granting the existence of such a fundamental law, it still cannot satisfactorily explain fine-tuning. There are two major reasons for this. First, the mathematical form of such a law would likely be a second-order (or higher-order) differential equation. While such a law might explain the fine-tuning of physical laws and fundamental constants, it would not specify the initial conditions of the universe. Thus, even if the law accounted for the fine-tuning of constants, the fine-tuning of initial conditions would remain unexplained. Second, a fundamental law that forces the constants of nature to take life-permitting values merely shifts the problem of fine-tuning. Instead of explaining the fine-tuning of the constants themselves, the fine-tuning would now apply to the fundamental law. The existence of a fundamental law that compels life-permitting constants is just as surprising as the constants themselves being fine-tuned by chance. Therefore, the puzzle of design remains unresolved.

3.5.2 The Appeal to a Multiverse

The most popular naturalistic response to the fine-tuning argument is that there are many universes, possibly infinitely many, each with different physical laws, initial conditions, and constants. Most of these universes cannot sustain life, but some can – and we happen to live in one of those. Proponents of the multiverse sometimes claim that it sufficiently explains fine-tuning without appeal to a designer.

There are several different models of the multiverse, and those which can be offered to explain fine-tuning can be classified threefold: as a Spatial Multiverse, a Temporal Multiverse, and a Metaphysical Multiverse.

---

[23] This objection resembles Larry Laudan's argument against scientific realism known as "Pessimistic Meta-Induction" (Laudan, 1981).

A Spatial Multiverse, the most popular, holds that we have a very large – perhaps infinitely large – single space multiverse, subdivided into smaller physical domains (i.e., universes). Each domain has different physical laws and constants. The most famous example of this kind of multiverse is Andrei Linde's chaotic inflation hypothesis (Linde, 1994) which we met in section 1. The main idea of this model is that we have a large, eternally expanding space, within which quantum effects continuously spawn new universes, which look like bubbles coming out of a bath. String theory holds that these bubbles to have different laws as well as initial conditions.

A Temporal Multiverse is a set of universes which exist in different temporally successive periods of time. Such models exhibit a single oscillating universe which expands and then collapses. In each expansion the universe starts with different sets of constants and initial conditions. The Steinhardt-Turok Ekpyrotic model and Penrose's conformal cyclic model are examples of this type of multiverse. In the Steinhardt-Turok Ekpyrotic model (Steinhardt & Turok, 2004), named after the ancient Stoic concept of *ekpyrosis* (cosmic destruction and rebirth), two parallel M-branes collide periodically in some higher dimensional space. These collisions correspond to a big bang, and the universe initiates expansion. Expansion is then reversed by contraction. In this model our universe lies on one of these two branes. As can be seen, this model heavily relies on super-string theory and extra dimensionality. Penrose's Conformal cyclic model (Penrose, 2006), based on general relativity, treats black holes as entropy eaters. Once all the black holes decay, and all matter decays to light, the entropy of the universe is lowered. When all of the temporal and spatial scales associated with the universe disappear, a new big bang initiates and we pass to the next cycle.

Lastly, a metaphysical type of multiverse is a model where all the universes are spatiotemporally separated. While both temporal and spatial multiverses involve some kind of physical mechanism through which these universes are created, a metaphysical multiverse lacks such mechanisms: the existence of these universes is taken as a brute fact. David Lewis's modal realism (Lewis, 2001) and Max Tegmark's fourth-level multiverse (Tegmark, 2005) are examples of metaphysical multiverses. These models predict an infinite number of universes. According to Lewisian modal realism, all of the possible universes exist; according to Tegmark, every mathematically consistent universe exists. These models are similar to each other, in that all possibilities are taken to be real.

As we will see in the next section, the multiverse hypothesis is consistent with Islamic thought and therefore need not conflict with the idea of design. It is important to note, however, that most multiverse models assume that all universes share the same fundamental constants and physical laws. In such cases, the multiverse does not constitute a range of universes with varying parameters, and thus cannot account for why our universe's constants are finely tuned for life.

For instance, in the Many-Worlds Interpretation of quantum mechanics (also known as the Everettian Multiverse), the various branches of the universal wavefunction correspond to different outcomes of quantum events, but the underlying laws and constants remain the same in every branch. Likewise, eternal inflation models that do not involve a varying landscape cannot explain fine-tuning for a similar reason: if the inflationary process were governed by a single inflation potential that does not permit significant variation in the resulting low-energy constants, then all observable regions would exhibit nearly identical physics. The inflation is a hypothetical scalar field thought to drive the rapid exponential expansion of space during the early universe. Its potential energy determines the dynamics of inflation and, in some models, the resulting physical properties of each region.

Only a small subset of multiverse models includes mechanisms that vary the constants of nature. These are the models that have the potential to explain the fine-tuning we observe in our universe.

Nevertheless, there are several reasons to question the explanatory adequacy of multiverse models that posit varying constants. One such concern is that they may commit what philosophers call the *inverse gambler's fallacy* (Hacking, 1987; White, 2000). Suppose a gambler enters a room and replaces a player in a poker hand, having no idea how many hands have been played before. He is dealt four aces and, struck by the improbability of this hand, concludes that many hands must have been played earlier. This reasoning is fallacious, since each hand is both equally probable and statistically independent of those played before.

Some philosophers, such as Roger White (2000), argue that a similar fallacy can arise in multiverse reasoning. Observing that our universe has the "winning hand" of life-permitting constants does not, by itself, justify concluding that countless other universes must exist. Without independent evidence for those universes, invoking them solely to explain fine-tuning risks circularity: the existence of many universes is "inferred" from the very phenomenon it is supposed to explain. Thus, while probabilistic reasoning is appropriate in ensemble contexts, the legitimacy of applying it here depends crucially on whether the multiverse itself is independently justified.

But even if we assume that explanations based on the multiverse do not commit the inverse gambler's fallacy, the multiverse still cannot solve the fine-tuning problem, as it merely shifts the question back one level to what has been called the multiverse generator – the physical mechanism responsible for producing the ensemble of universes. If a naturalistic multiverse exists, some physical mechanism must create both spatial and temporal universes. This multiverse generator mechanism must satisfy several conditions such that universes with different constants and initial conditions can be formed. Taking chaotic inflation as an example, it must satisfy the following conditions, as explained by Robin Collins:

> consider the inflationary type multiverse generator. In order for it to explain the fine-tuning of the constants, it must hypothesize one or more "mechanisms" or laws that will do the following five things: (i) cause the expansion of a small region of space into a very large region; (ii) generate the very large amount of mass-energy needed for that region to contain matter instead of merely empty space; (iii) convert the mass energy of inflated space to the sort of mass-energy we find in our universe; and (iv) cause sufficient variations among the constants of physics to explain their fine-tuning. (Collins, 2009: 263)

Thus, even if we assume that there is some multiverse generator, which creates universes with different constants and initial conditions, the multiverse generator itself must be fine-tuned. Since, if any of the aforementioned laws governing this universe generator were lacking, it would not have been able to produce hospitable universes. Using Collins's example of a bread-making machine, in order to make bread, the machine must function properly: it must have a suitable electrical system, it must produce the right temperature, it must set the correct time, and it requires you to have entered the ingredients of the bread in the right order and the right proportion. Thus, even a bread generator must be well designed, and given that the universe generator will be much more complex, surely it will require many specific conditions to function adequately.

There is one important further problem for all varieties of multiverse, particularly the infinite ones, which is worth mentioning. According to quantum statistical physics, there is a nonzero probability that a fully formed brain may pop out of a vacuum with false memories and perceptions. Such brains are called Boltzmann brains. It is perfectly possible that we are Boltzmann brains rather than normal human beings. Of course, the probability of the emergence of a Boltzmann brain is extremely low, so if we are living in a single universe, then we can be confident that we are not Boltzmann brains (Page, 2008). But if we are living in a multiverse, then, since the emergence of Boltzmann brains do not require fine-tuning, they will emerge even in universes that are not suitable for life. Hence, in a multiverse it is extremely more likely that we are hallucinating Boltzmann brains. So, not only do nontheistic multiverse proponents face a fine-tuning challenge, they also face the Boltzmann brain problem – that it is statistically more likely that we ourselves are Boltzmann brains, experiencing illusory memories and perceptions. This, of course, would undermine our ability to trust observational data and perform science reliably. This concern is explored in greater detail in the following section, where I contrast the implications for naturalistic versus theistic interpretations of the multiverse.

Modern physics shows that our universe is finely tuned for life. After examining alternative naturalistic explanations and finding them wanting, the design hypothesis appears more convincing. Thus, the best explanation for fine-tuning seems to be a cosmic designer, which strongly supports theism.

3.6 Fine-Tuning for Discoverability

In this section, we turn to a less frequently discussed but profoundly intriguing aspect of fine-tuning: the fine-tuning of the universe for discoverability and technological advancement. In the 2010s, physicist and philosopher Robin Collins proposed that the universe is not only fine-tuned for the emergence of life, but also for the pursuit of scientific discovery and the development of technology (Collins, 2018). That is, the fundamental constants, laws, and parameters of nature appear to be set at values that make the universe amenable to systematic exploration and technological innovation.

To say the universe is fine-tuned for discoverability is to suggest that relatively minor deviations in these parameters would render scientific inquiry far more difficult, if not altogether impossible. Similarly, the claim that the universe is fine-tuned for technology holds that its physical structure is remarkably suited to the development and functioning of technological systems, and that modest changes in physical constants would preclude such advancements.

Consider, for instance, the electromagnetic force that binds electrons to atomic nuclei. This interaction is governed by the fine-structure constant. Were this constant increased by just 10 percent, combustion processes would be significantly impaired, preventing the sustained burning of fire. This would severely limit technological activities such as metalworking, which are foundational to scientific progress. Conversely, if the constant were slightly smaller, fires would burn uncontrollably, rapidly consuming all flammable material. In such an environment, the emergence of a civilization capable of developing science and technology would be highly improbable.

Moreover, a reduced fine-structure constant would diminish the resolving power of optical instruments like microscopes, making it impossible to observe small biological structures such as cells. Technological applications reliant on electromagnetism – such as transformers, electric motors, and antennas – would also be compromised.

Other forces illustrate similar points. If the weak nuclear force were ten times stronger, atomic decay rates would increase a hundredfold. Radiometric dating methods, such as potassium-argon and carbon-14 dating, would become unreliable or infeasible, undermining our ability to reconstruct historical timelines. A tenfold decrease in this force would render neutrinos undetectable, depriving us of crucial information about stellar processes.

Even the cosmic microwave background (CMB) radiation – our window into the early universe – depends sensitively on the baryon-to-photon ratio. Were this ratio an order of magnitude larger or smaller, the CMB would be undetectable, and the field of cosmology would suffer a severe epistemic loss.

These examples, among many others, underscore a remarkable and underappreciated fact: the physical parameters of our universe fall within narrow ranges that not only allow life, but also facilitate our capacity to explore, understand, and transform the environment through science and technology. The conjunction of these conditions is difficult to plausibly attribute to chance alone. A similar argument to that developed earlier in this section for the fine-tuning of life can thus be constructed on the basis of fine-tuning for discoverability and technology. In some respects, this version of the argument may be even more resilient to the standard multiverse objection, since many multiverse models focus exclusively on anthropic selection for life-permitting conditions, without guaranteeing that the resulting universes would also support scientific investigation or technological development. The intelligibility and tractability of the universe may therefore point to a deeper level of design than life-permitting structure alone.

3.7 From Precision to Presence: Fine-Tuning as a Theological and Spiritual Sign

The fine-tuning argument resembles Ibn Rushd's *Dalīl al-'Ināya*, examined earlier. While Ibn Rushd did not have access to modern cosmology or physics, his method closely parallels the logic of fine-tuning. Both begin with the observation that the universe is remarkably hospitable to life. Both argue that such suitability is not plausibly the result of chance. And both infer an intelligent, intentional designer as the best explanation.

Fine-tuning has also been explored by two notable Muslim physicists: Basil Altaie and Nidhal Guessoum. Altaie deepens the argument by interpreting the data of modern cosmology through two paired Qur'ānic principles. The first is *taqdīr*, the assertion claim that "everything with Him has a measure" – a motif that appears, for example, in *ar-Ra'd* (13:8), *al-Furqān* (25:2), and *al-Qamar (54:49)* (Altaie, 2019: 111–112). Yet precision alone is only half the story. The Qur'ān also insists that the heavens and the earth have been *taskhīr*-ed – "made subservient" – to humankind, as stated in *al-Jāthiyah* (45:13), *Luqmān* (31:20), and *an-Naḥl* (16:12). Because those same constants secure stable stellar furnaces, temperate planets, and the biochemical pathways on which rational life depends, Altaie sees their life-friendliness as the operational side of *taskhīr*: the universe is not merely measured; it is measured for a beneficiary, human beings (Altaie, 2019: 110–111). In this synthesis, *taqdīr* explains why the laws of nature exhibit such uncanny exactitude, while *taskhīr* discloses for whom that exactitude was engineered – integrating the fine-tuning argument into an explicitly Islamic theology of creation of humanity.

Guessoum likewise finds Qur'ānic language that resonates with cosmic fine-tuning, but he frames the connection with greater epistemic caution. He cites the claims that God "created everything and proportioned it in due measure" in *al-Furqān* (25:2) and that God "raised the heaven and set up the balance" (*ar-Raḥmān* (55:7) as scriptural expressions of *taqdīr* – a cosmic ordering whose empirical echo, he argues, lies in the calibrated physical constants discovered by modern physics (Guessoum, 2011: 269). Complementing this, he points to the refrain that the heavens and earth have been "made subservient" to humanity in *Luqmān* (31:20) as Islam's analogue to the anthropic principle. Yet, because the Qur'ān couples this subservience to a moral test rather than mere biological accommodation, Guessoum labels it an "ultra-anthropic principle" that centers the human ethical vocation within cosmic purpose (Guessoum, 2011: 264–265, 269). Thus, for Guessoum, fine-tuning signals divinely measured order (*taqdīr*), while *taskhīr* provides a providential frame – but any theological reading, he cautions, must be integrated with evolutionary cosmology and must avoid reducing science to mere proof-texts (Guessoum, 2011: 254).

The fine-tuning of the universe offers a compelling example of what Sufis describe as *Tawāfuq* – a term denoting harmonious coincidences or alignments that point to a divinely orchestrated order. Unlike traditional design arguments – which often rely on analogies drawn between human artifacts (such as a watch), on the one hand, and biological systems on the other – the fine-tuning argument gestures toward a grander scope. Fine-tuning points not to a local designer but to a cosmic one: an agent capable of calibrating the laws of nature and the values of fundamental constants. Such a designer is not confined to a particular location or mechanism within the universe but possesses the power to shape its very fabric. This implies a being of immense wisdom and power – rightly described as the Lord of the Cosmos.

To fine-tune a universe is to know not only the conditions under which life might emerge but also the conditions that would make life capable of cognition, exploration, and reflection. The universe's discoverability – its mathematical elegance, internal consistency, and responsiveness to rational inquiry – suggests that the designer values both life *and* mind. It implies that the emergence of conscious, reasoning beings was not an incidental byproduct but a meaningful objective – of a personal God who is not only the sustainer of life but also the ground of meaning, contemplation, and inner life.

The fact that everyday objects – and even our own bodies – are governed by the same finely tuned laws and constants that make life possible takes on deeper significance when viewed through a Sufi lens. In this tradition, which emphasizes inner purification and direct experiential knowledge of the Divine, the cosmos is not merely a physical construct but a spiritual signpost. The finely calibrated order of the universe is a cosmic *āyah* – a divine sign – calling not only for intellectual assent but also for spiritual attentiveness. From the Sufi perspective, creation serves both a functional and symbolic purpose, inviting the human being into *tafakkur* (contemplation) and *taḥqīq* (spiritual realization). The delicate balance required for the emergence of life and mind reflects a deeper calling: just as the cosmos is harmonized for flourishing, so too are we called to fine-tune our inner lives – to align our desires, thoughts, and actions with divine order. It is a reminder that God's wisdom exceeds human comprehension, urging not domination but *tawakkul* (trustful surrender) to divine governance. The universe, then, is not only *taskhīr*-ed – made subservient – for our physical survival or scientific inquiry, but also for our spiritual ascent. In this view, its discoverability and mathematical elegance are not just tools for knowing the world but are also tools for knowing the Divine. The constancy of physical laws across all of space is a reflection of God's constancy, a mirror in which we are invited to perceive the "face of God," as alluded to in *al-Baqarah* (2:115). Gratitude (*shukr*), then, is the requisite response to such cosmic grace. Everything in the universe is an *āyah* – a sign – calling the seeker toward God. Thus, from the Sufi vantage point, fine-tuning is not merely evidence for a cosmic designer; it is an invitation to inner awakening and the realization of the divine presence woven into the fabric of existence.

4 Lord of the Worlds: Exploring the Multiverse in an Islamic Context

As we saw in the previous section, the most popular naturalistic response to the fine-tuning argument is the multiverse hypothesis. Proponents of this view claim the multiverse hypothesis sufficiently explains fine-tuning without appeal to a designer, which leads certain theists and atheists to regard the multiverse as a threat to rational theism: if the multiverse were actual, they contend, it would render God superfluous.[24]

Some philosophers, on the other hand, argue that the multiverse is not only opposed to theism, it is useful to theism. For example, some theists deploy the multiverse in support of theodicies (Turner, 2003), arguing that God may allow suffering or imperfection in individual universes because, across a multiverse, greater goods or divine purposes are realized that justify such instances of evil. Others claim that God would create every possible universe in which good outweighs evil. On this view, the multiverse, taken collectively, is the best possible world, since it maximizes total goodness across all morally permissible realities. As such, the multiverse offers a response to the "best possible world" objection – namely, the challenge of explaining why a perfect God did not create a better world than the one we observe (Kraay, 2010).

As a Muslim philosopher and physicist who is open to the idea of a multiverse, I hold that Islamic theism, under certain assumptions, implies some form of multiverse. Adhering to the principle of "mere Islam" outlined in the second section, I will not endorse any single intellectual tradition. While I personally identify with the *Ḥanafī-Māturīdī* school, I set aside that affiliation in order to engage a broader range of Islamic perspectives. Indeed, the arguments for *Multiverse Theism* that follow are intended to remain accessible and relevant across different theological frameworks. I intend for these arguments to resonate with various Islamic schools of thought, offering each community compelling reasons that align with its doctrine. While I may critique certain schools in specific sections, my broader objective is to remain inclusive and respectful of differing viewpoints. Throughout this discussion, I will use the term *Multiverse Theism* to denote the stance that upholds both Islamic theism and the multiverse hypothesis.

I will also not tie the term "multiverse" to any one model but remain open-minded about its specific features except those required by our arguments. My goal is to show that, under Islamic theism, Multiverse Theism is both a plausible and a non–ad hoc invention. I will argue that a Muslim theologian has independent and credible reasons to believe in a multiverse. Consequently, if the multiverse were to become firmly established scientific theory, it would offer modest support for Islamic theism.

Hence, the multiverse concept is neither a challenge to rational faith in God nor a last-minute contrivance to "rescue" theism from scientific advancement. In fact, the Qur'an provides theological insights – potentially not fully

---

[24] For physicists defending this claim see: (Susskind, 2005; Green, 2011; Tegmark, 2014). For philosophers defending the claim that fine-tuning can be explained via multiverse see: (Leslie, 1989; Smart, 1989; Parfit, 1998: 24–27; Bradley, 2009: 61–72).

appreciable until the rise of Einsteinian physics and quantum mechanics – that point toward the multiverse. The Qur'an states:

> God it is who has created seven heavens, and a similar number of earths. The commandments come down among them slowly, that you may know that God is able to do all things, and that God surrounds all things in knowledge. (*al-Ṭalāq*, 65:12)

While this verse does not conclusively indicate a multiverse, it clearly suggests a plurality of "heavens and earths" (with "seven" possibly signifying perfection). Its inclusion in Islam's foundational text thus undermines the claim that the multiverse is a theologically ad hoc proposal.[25]

Furthermore, in the opening chapter of the Qur'an and in the daily prayers that Muslims have recited from the start, one finds the proclamation:

> Praise be to Allah, the Cherisher and Sustainer of the worlds (*al-Fātiḥah*, 1:2).

While "worlds" (*al-'ālamīn*) has traditionally been interpreted to include both physical and supernatural realms, it could also be read – especially in light of modern cosmology – as referring to distinct, spatiotemporally independent domains. In this sense, the concept may resonate with the idea of a multiverse. Indeed, the Qur'an frequently addresses Allah as the Lord of the Worlds.

Additional theological support for Multiverse Theism emerges from fairly common Islamic interpretations and extensions of core divine attributes. Islam's case for a multiverse can be split into two main strands. The first is grounded in the divine attribute of everlastingness. Certain medieval Muslim thinkers proposed that since some of God's attributes manifest themselves in creation and are everlasting, the universe must also be everlasting. The unification of these medieval insights with the modern revelation that our universe has a finite past suggests the plausibility of a multiverse. The second strand is rooted in "perfect being" theology: if some of God's attributes are reflected in creation, and God possesses every possible perfection, then one might anticipate a creation with maximum scope. In other words, God's attributes combine to present a theological rationale for a multiverse.

In the following sections, I will examine both lines of argument in greater detail.[26]

---

[25] It is important to note that multiple alternative readings of (*al-Ṭalāq*, 65:12) exist that need not involve the multiverse. In its commentary, the Turkish Directorate of Religious Affairs highlights various understandings of "seven earths," including the cosmology known during the Prophet's time, references to seven continents, a notion of seven separate planets, or seven layers of the earth. Additionally, the number "seven" may function symbolically to convey perfection or plurality, rather than a specific count (Karaman et al., 2020: vol. 5, 396–397).

[26] The arguments presented here are based on: (Doko, 2024).

4.1 Arguments Grounded in God's Role as Creator

4.1.1 The Argument from God's Everlasting Attribute of Creating

The first argument stems from God's role as creator. In classical Islamic theism, God is the originator and sustainer of everything, and being creator (*al-Khāliq*) is an essential divine attribute (*al-An'ām*, 6:102; *al-Ra'd*, 13:16; *Yā Sīn*, 36:81; *al-Zumar*, 39:62; *Ghāfir*, 40:62; *al-Ḥashr*, 59:24). In this view, God brought all that exists into being, out of nothing and without a prior example. With the exception of the emanation model we discussed in the second section, all creation models accept this view.

Drawing on the creator attribute, one might propose the following argument in favor of a multiverse:

1. God is *everlastingly* the creator.
2. In order to be called "creator," one must have created something.
3. God created our universe, which has a finite past.
4. From (1) and (3), God was a creator before bringing our universe into being.
5. Therefore, God created another universe prior to ours (and another prior to that universe, *ad infinitum*).
6. Consequently, theism suggests a multiverse.

Because these points involve numerous metaphysical assumptions – some of which we will address shortly – this is not offered as definitive, deductive proof that Islamic theism implies a multiverse. Nevertheless, if premises (1)–(5) are not inherently implausible, then Islamic theism fits well with the concept of a multiverse.

The first premise maintains that being creator is one of God's essential attributes, implying that God has always been the creator (a being that is not creator cannot be God). This can be understood in two ways. One interpretation is that God is eternal – existing outside of time, experiencing all events in a single, timeless moment, thus possessing all divine attributes in a timeless state (including being the creator). Another interpretation is that God is everlasting – has always existed and will always exist – but with experiences unfolding in temporal succession. The arguments in this first category assume that God is everlasting. As such, it aligns with Ibn Taymiyyah's model of creation discussed in the second section, which, based on a literal reading of the Qur'an, assumes that God is everlasting.

The second premise states that to manifest the attribute of a creator, one must have engaged in an act of creation. Calling someone a "creator" implies having actually created something that did not exist before. This distinction is crucial: possessing the potential to create is not the same as being a creator. A person may have every skill and tool needed to paint, but until they have completed a painting, they are not a painter.

The third premise asserts that our universe has a finite past. This idea is widely accepted among theists; in Islamic theism – particularly within the orthodox Ash'ari and Maturidi traditions as we discussed in the second section – the universe is said to have been brought into existence ex nihilo by divine command, thus implying a finite temporal history. All of the Islamic creation models discussed in the second section, with the exception of the emanation model, naturally align with this premise.

From these three premises, the rest of the argument follows: if God is everlastingly the creator, then God must already have been a creator prior to forming our universe. And if being a creator requires having created something, God must have brought into existence something else before creating our universe.

Several objections can be raised against the argument earlier. One is that God may be the everlasting creator by virtue of creating nonspatial, nontemporal entities – namely, abstract objects – prior to creating our universe. In this view, God's status as creator predates our universe, not because He made a prior universe or multiple universes, but because He (everlastingly) brings abstract objects into existence. This objection, however, depends on Theistic Activism – the view that abstract entities like moral truths or mathematical facts are created by God's will (Morris & Menzel, 1986: 353–362). This view has been widely contested, particularly due to what is known as the bootstrapping problem: if God creates necessary truths, then it seems He must already possess certain attributes (such as rationality or logical understanding) that themselves presuppose those truths. Critics argue this results in a circular explanation, undermining the coherence of Theistic Activism (Gould, 2011: 255–274). Moreover, creation seems to involve a temporal sequence – a "before" and an "after." If abstract objects are outside of time, the very ideas of "before" and "after" would not apply to them, making their "creation" incoherent. Consequently, this challenge is weak.

A second objection targets the second premise by asserting that for God to be the creator, He need not actually have created anything – merely possessing the ability to create is enough to be called creator. However, this view fails to distinguish between the attribute of "creator" and that of "omnipotence," which is God's power to create. One could conceive of an omnipotent being that never brings anything into existence, yet we would not call that being a creator. By definition, a creator must have created.

Another avenue is to reject the third premise. One might propose that the universe itself is eternal, with God acting as creator by continually sustaining or recreating it at every instant of its endless existence. While this idea is not strictly incompatible with Islam in general, as discussed in the second section, it clashes with the particular orthodox Muslim conviction that only God is everlasting. Claiming that God perpetually creates a single eternal universe could still fit within Islamic theism if this creation is understood as a sequence of finite universes across time – an eternal chain of temporally bounded universes, with ours just the most recent. Here, no universe is everlasting; only God is. This "recreation model" hints at a temporal multiverse. Under that assumption, the argument's conclusion remains intact. I will return to the question of whether an everlasting multiverse poses a challenge to Islamic orthodox theology later.

One might worry that the premise, "God alone is everlasting," conflicts with our central argument. As an objection, it could be said that if God is the only everlasting being, there must be a moment, call it t, before which only God exists, with no other entity (including universes). This seems at odds with God's identity as an everlasting creator and might undermine the argument based on that attribute. Yet contending that God is the only everlasting being does not require pinpointing a time t at which God was entirely alone. Precisely because God is an everlasting creator, at any given moment t, God would already have brought some universe – call it universe$_t$ – into existence. Does this undermine God's solitary everlastingness? Not necessarily. For each time t and its universe$_t$, there is a preceding moment $t-1$ when that universe did not exist, while God did. No universe is beginningless or exists at every conceivable moment. All universes have starting points; God does not. Hence, God precedes every universe He creates. It is true that for any time t, there may be infinitely many universes, but as long as each one has a beginning and a prior period of nonexistence, no contradiction arises.

A related concern is that such reasoning implies an everlasting multiverse, thereby positing two eternal "beings": God and the multiverse. This raises a theological red flag in orthodox Islamic thought, where *Tawḥīd* implies that no other eternal entity exists alongside God.[27] To resolve this, it is important to clarify that the multiverse is not truly a "being" in its own right – it is merely a term describing a collection of distinct, finite universes. It has no existence beyond its individual components and thus lacks any properties of its own. Consequently, there is no entity alongside God that is co-everlasting. Several points support the idea that the multiverse is not a single entity. Mereology, the study of parts and wholes, suggests that distinct entities form a unified whole only if they share significant relational or interactive properties. In a multiverse

---

[27] For a more nuanced discussion of this issue, including Ibn Rushd's view that an eternal creation does not violate divine uniqueness, see Sections 2.4 and 2.5.

setup, separate universes are causally disconnected, lacking any interactions or bonds to merge them into a new "whole." Moreover, Occam's Razor advises against adding unnecessary entities without a commensurate gain in explanatory power. Suggesting that the multiverse, independent of individual universes, constitutes a genuine being complicates matters without offering additional insight. By treating it merely as a collective label for multiple unconnected universes, we adhere to conceptual simplicity and avoid unnecessary metaphysical baggage.[28]

In summary, classical Islamic views of God as essentially creator, combined with the notion of an everlasting deity and the rejection of Theistic Activism's account of eternal creation, lend considerable plausibility to a multiverse scenario.

4.1.2 The Argument from the Best Creator

By drawing on God's role as creator and the principles of perfect being theology, one can construct an Islamic argument for Multiverse Theism:

1. God possesses every great-making attribute in its maximal form.
2. God is the creator.
3. A being who brings into existence all universes worthy of creation is superior to one who makes only a single universe.
4. Therefore, God brings into existence all worthy universes, that is, a multiverse.

The first premise reiterates the central idea of perfect being theology, while the second premise aligns with Islamic theism. Since God is the most perfect being, God possesses all compatible great-making qualities to the highest degree. Hence, if God's nature is to create, then God is not only a creator but the best possible creator. This accords with the Islamic understanding of God, as the best creator: "So exalted be Allah, the best of creators" (*al-Mu'minūn*, 23:14).

The third premise captures the idea that, other things being equal, a being who creates multiple worthwhile entities is a "better creator"[29] than one who only creates a single entity. Consequently, the creation must be unsurpassable. Because our universe alone can be outdone – by imagining a cosmos containing

---

[28] The remark that universes are prior to the multiverse needs additional defense, since some models of multiverse seem to imply that there are meta-laws above the universes. For example, universes in the Quantum Mechanical multiverse are connected by and evolve according to the universal wavefunction. This can be used as an argument against the claim that universes are prior to the multiverse.

[29] Intuitively, not every creation is worth creating, such as evilverses: universes in which it is just evil or evil suppresses goodness. We should note the adjective better refers to the creative power of, rather than the axiological degree of the creation.

two universes, or three, or four, and so on – the ultimate reality would be a multiverse, comprising both our own universe and other axiologically valuable universes (i.e., universes that are good or worthwhile to create (1879–1955)). This "multiverse," with more moral agents, more energy, and more space and time, is superior to any single universe. Therefore, the creator of such a multiverse would surpass the creator of a single universe.

One might argue that only a single universe is worth creating, which challenges the third premise. This objection will be addressed in the next section.

In sum, by synthesizing perfect being theology with the divine attribute of creator, the case for a multiverse strengthens.

4.2 Arguments from the Moral Attributes of God

4.2.1 The Argument from the Moral Perfection of God

Within Islam, God is understood to be perfectly good, as illustrated by the divine name *Al-Barr* (*al-Ṭūr*, 52:28). Because goodness is essential to God's nature, one would expect God to maximize, as far as logically possible, the moral and aesthetic value of reality. Guided by this principle, numerous thinkers – including Ibn Sīnā (Ibn Sina, 1968–1971: 158–160), al-Ghazālī (al-Ghazālī, 2001: 47–50), Ibn Taymiyyah (Hoover, 2004), Ibn ʿArabī (Chittick, 1989: 289–301), and Leibniz (Caro, 2020) – have maintained that God created the best possible world. Ibn Sīnā, who likely introduced this idea into Islamic thought, claimed that God is "a cause in Itself of good and perfection insofar as that is possible" (Ibn Sina, 1960: 415). Al-Ghazālī similarly wrote, "There is not in possibility more wonderful than this world, because of the perfected existence of all realities within it" (Ormsby, 1984: 106). While this view is not widely embraced by the dominant *Ashʿarī* school of Muslim theology, it appears among some Sufis, influenced in part by the mystical works of Ibn ʿArabī (Ormsby, 1984: 103–107).

Building on this concept, some contemporary philosophers argue that the best possible "world" is in fact a multiverse (Kraay, 2010: 355–368). Likewise, Paul Draper proposes that a God with unlimited creative resources and perfect goodness is likely to bring about a multiverse (Draper, 2004: 311–321). In the following discussion, we develop and defend an Islamic formulation of this argument for Multiverse Theism.

Those who base their case for a theistic multiverse on God's perfect goodness often suggest that God creates every universe where the overall good outweighs the evil (up to some nonarbitrary threshold). We remain agnostic about the precise nature of that threshold. Instead, we define "universes worth creating" as any universe that God would select to enhance the total goodness of reality. We then refer to the case from God's moral perfection for a multiverse in the following terms:

1. God is all good.
2. God is omnipotent.
3. All good beings would increase the value of reality.
4. A universe worth creating (i.e., one that enhances the total goodness of reality) increases the value of reality.
5. An omnipotent being can create any universe worth creating.
6. Therefore, God would create any universe worth creating.
7. Therefore, there is more than one possible universe.
8. Therefore, God would create more than one universe.
9. Therefore, God would create a multiverse.

Under the framework of Islamic theism, there is little dispute about the first two premises. The third premise naturally arises from God's essential goodness. The fourth premise relies on the standard assumption that value is additive; that is, when you have two distinct universes, their combined overall value is at least as great as the value of either universe in isolation. The fifth premise follows from the nature of divine omnipotence, presuming that these universes are internally consistent and align with correct counterfactuals of freedom (i.e., hypothetical truths about what free creatures would freely choose under various conditions). Consequently, the sixth premise builds on the previous ones.

The seventh premise is also plausible; there is no obvious reason to think that just one universe merits creation. For instance, if universe U1 is worth creating, then another universe U2 – identical to U1 but containing one additional neutrino – would very likely be worth creating. While it is theoretically possible that such a minor change could have unforeseen consequences, it would be surprising if only one precise configuration (among countless near-variants) were non-chaotic or morally valuable. Combining the sixth and seventh premises then leads to the conclusion that a multiverse exists.

A possible concern is to deny that objective values exist or that they can be attributed to reality. However, this stance holds little appeal for Muslims, who believe that God endows reality with objective values. Certainly, critics who reject God's existence might also reject objective values, but our argument begins with the premise of Islamic theism, which maintains or implies that creation possess objective value.

Some extreme forms of *Divine Voluntarism* – the view that moral value is entirely determined by God's will – possibly found in certain interpretations of the *Ash'arī* tradition, may also question the third premise of our argument.

Those who adopt such a view may find the argument less persuasive. In the next section, I will briefly critique this more radical strand of divine voluntarism.

Denying the existence of objective values would also weaken atheism's strongest argument against theism: the problem of evil. If universes do not have objective value, then moral distinctions between "good" and "evil" are incoherent – rendering the concept of divine goodness meaningless. In such a framework, God – while still called "good" – could create any kind or amount of suffering or disorder without contradiction, since these categories would lack any objective basis.

A Muslim might still object that God's creative decision is not bound by maximizing value, pointing out that God, being maximally free, could create based on criteria unrelated to moral value (or without any criteria at all). This objection faces two difficulties. First, it is unclear what other, non-axiological standard an all-good God might use. An essentially good being would presumably not disregard moral value in favor of creating a world governed by random factors like an even count of objects or an abundance of the color purple. Although God could theoretically do so, it seems contrary to essential divine goodness. Hence, it makes more sense to interpret God's freedom as guided by His essential attributes. Second, any non-axiological criteria that God employed would still yield a multiverse. In principle, one could adapt the argument accordingly – there would still be infinitely many possible universes with an even number of objects or featuring vast amounts of purple. Regardless of the criterion – moral or otherwise – one would again anticipate a multiverse.

Another objection posits that God's criteria are met uniquely by our universe, so that only one universe is created, being the best under those criteria. Yet this scenario is difficult to justify because we can imagine a universe identical to ours but with one additional neutrino, which would presumably be of equal or greater value and thus similarly worth creating.

To summarize, the idea of an all-good, omnipotent God who invests universes with objective value, coupled with the assumption that value is cumulative, naturally leans toward the multiverse hypothesis.

4.2.2 The Argument from No Perfect Universe

Fakhr al-Dīn al-Rāzī contended that our current world cannot be "the perfect world" because, much like searching for the largest possible number, aiming for the largest or best or most perfect world is impossible (al-Razi, 1987: 107). Where there is no upper limit, one can always envision something better or bigger: for instance, God could add more righteous people to a given world (while proportionally expanding its size), thereby improving it. Consequently, the very notion of a "perfect world" is, according to many contemporary philosophers, incoherent. This viewpoint has been advanced by modern scholars such as Plantinga (Plantinga, 1974: 61), Swinburne (Swinburne, 1979: 114–115), Forrest (Forrest, 1981: 49–54), Schlesinger (Schlesinger, 1977), Reichenbach (Reichenbach, 1982: 121–129), and Rubio (Rubio, 2020).

From this, one cannot escape the fact that, for any world God might choose, there is a conceivable world that is better. William Rowe observes that this poses a dilemma for a Perfect Being (Rowe, 1994), implying that God could be morally surpassed – if God can always do better, then God would not be the greatest conceivable being. Intriguingly, however, Rowe's argument can be reframed into an argument for Multiverse Theism:

1. For any given universe, there is a better possible universe.
2. If God were to create a single universe, his work would be morally surpassable.
3. God is the greatest possible being.
4. If God is the greatest possible being, then God's work cannot be morally surpassable.
5. God's work is not morally surpassable.
6. Therefore, God did not create a single universe.
7. God created at least one universe.
8. Therefore, God created a multiverse.

The first premise extends the "no best world" reasoning to universes, asserting an unending scale of ever-improving universes. The second premise follows naturally: if this infinite spectrum exists, then for any universe God creates, there will always be a superior universe left uncreated. The third premise relies on Perfect Being Theology, and the fourth premise flows logically from it. In turn, the fifth premise stems from the third and fourth, and the sixth premise is derived from the second and fifth. When you combine the sixth premise with the fact that God created our universe, it implies that God created a multiverse. Although the argument is presented in a deductive framework, we acknowledge the difficulty in substantiating all its premises or accounting for any potentially relevant but unconsidered premises.

Daniel and Frances Howard-Snyder (Howard-Snyder & Howard-Snyder, 1994: 260–268) reject the fourth premise, maintaining that the creation of a perfect being can be morally surpassable. They illustrate this with the example of two perfect beings who rely on a random-selection mechanism to determine which universe to create. Suppose one being produces a universe superior to the other's. Does this mean that the first being is surpassed by the second? Because both relied on the same random process, the Howard-Snyders argue, there is no basis to claim that one perfect being outperformed the other. Therefore, having a surpassable creation does not imply that a perfect being can be surpassed.

However, their argument appears to assume that God (or a perfect being) is limited to creating only one universe. They hint at this when describing the second omnipotent being, who "did not create them all." If it were possible for an omnipotent creator to produce all morally desirable universes, then choosing a single universe would suggest some shortcoming in divine goodness. Under a single-universe framework, perhaps omnipotence did the best it could. Yet if the multiverse is feasible, that conclusion may not hold. Any solitary universe would be morally overshadowed by a multiverse – exactly the sort of creation one might expect from the greatest conceivable being.

Another objection could involve modifying Rowe's stance to claim that there cannot be a "best possible multiverse" because one could always imagine a still-better multiverse. While this line of reasoning may apply to certain physical theories of the multiverse, it does not necessarily affect the theological multiverse at issue here. In the theological view, the multiverse encompasses all universes worth creating, leaving no room for a "better" multiverse.

4.2.3 The Argument from the Highest Love

Under classical Islamic theism, God is understood to be perfectly loving – *Al-Wadūd* (*Hūd*, 11:90; *al-Burūj*, 85:14) – which is one of the ninety-nine essential divine attributes in Islamic theology. From the standpoint of Perfect Being Theology, this implies that God's love is unparalleled: we cannot conceive of a being more loving than God. Consequently, it follows that God would create every being that is worthy of love. This reasoning can be summarized as follows:

1. We cannot imagine a more loving being than God.
2. In order to truly love, an object of love must exist at some time t or timelessly.
3. A being B1 who loves more beings than a being B2 (with the same degree of love) is more loving than B2.
4. If God were not to create all the beings worthy of love, we could imagine a more loving being than God.
5. God creates all the beings worthy of love.
6. Not all beings worth loving exist in our universe.
7. God created a multiverse.

The first premise is the theological assertion that God is the epitome of love. The second premise follows naturally from the first and from Perfect Being

Theology. The third premise states that genuine love necessitates the actual (past, present, or future) existence of the beloved. For instance, one can love a person who no longer exists (like a deceased grandparent) or who does not yet exist (an unborn child). What one cannot do, according to this premise, is truly love a being that never has existed and never will.

The fourth premise assumes that, like moral value, love is "additive." If one loves more individuals (with the same degree of love), one is, in that sense, more loving. It is akin to saying that someone who loves every member of her family is more loving than someone who loves just one child. From the third and fourth premises, we arrive at the fifth: if God failed to create all love-worthy beings, we could conceive of a yet more loving being (simply by envisioning one that created an additional person, all else being equal).

The sixth premise then follows: because God is the supreme loving being – and because true love requires the beloved to exist – God creates all who merit love. Since clearly not all such beings are found in our universe, God must have created a multiverse.

Naturally, this argument is speculative and open to numerous objections. One such objection challenges the third premise, suggesting that it is indeed possible to love nonexistent beings (for example, certain people say they love fictional characters). However, one may reply that while you can feel affection for imaginary entities, such a sentiment may not qualify as love. Proper love typically involves sharing what one has for the other's good, something that requires the beloved's existence.

4.3 Arguments from the Lord Attribute of God

In this section, we briefly outline two further arguments – one stemming from the concept of an everlasting God and another from Perfect-Being Theology – without offering detailed replies to potential objections. Among God's essential names in Islamic tradition is Ar-Rabb, frequently rendered as "The Lord." In this context, "Lord" (Rabb) refers to one who has authority, care, and sovereignty over subjects capable of response or obedience. Of course, the attribute of lordship is not exclusive to Islam; all theistic religions recognize God as Lord. Aquinas, for instance, posits that one can infer the world's eternity from God's "Lord from eternity" attribute (Davidson, 1987: 64). We can adapt that idea into an argument for Multiverse Theism:

1. God is everlastingly the Lord.
2. A being can be a Lord only if there is a subject over whom he has authority.
3. God created our universe, that is, our universe has a finite past.
4. God was the Lord before He created our universe.

5. Thus, God must have created some other universe before our universe.
6. Therefore, theism implies a multiverse.

Like the earlier argument based on God's everlastingness, this reasoning presupposes that God is eternal and that our universe began at some finite point in time. The second premise is plausible because "Lord" suggests having authority over entities capable of responding – meaning abstract objects cannot qualify as subjects. Thus, "Lord" entails dominion over beings who can submit or obey, reinforcing the notion that God could have ruled over other universes before ours.

One can also construct an argument based on Perfect Being Theology using God's lordship. If God is the greatest conceivable being, then God must also be the greatest conceivable Lord. Furthermore, a lord who governs more subjects is, by that measure, a greater lord than one who oversees fewer. Therefore, if God truly is the greatest possible Lord, one would expect Him to create all beings whose existence remains consistent with His other attributes – implying a multiverse. This can be outlined as follows:

1. God is the greatest conceivable being.
2. God is the greatest possible Lord.
3. If being, B1, is in authority over more subjects than being, B2, then B1 is a greater Lord than B2.
4. If God did not create all beings worth creating, we could imagine a greater being than God.
5. Therefore, God created all beings worth creating.
6. Not all beings worth creating exist in our universe.
7. God created a multiverse.

The first two premises rest on the foundations of Perfect Being Theology, and the fourth follows from the third; the fifth follows from the earlier statements. The sixth premise is self-evidently true, while the only truly contentious point is the third premise, which is simply a slightly stronger version of the second premise from the previous argument. Intuitively, it seems that a lord with more subjects would be considered a higher or greater lord.

4.4 Boltzmann Brain Problem in Multiverse Theism

In the previous section, we briefly touched on the "Boltzmann Brain" problem in the context of a multiverse.[30] The core idea is that random quantum or thermal fluctuations might generate numerous short-lived, self-aware entities –

---

[30] For a detailed discussion of the Boltzmann Brain problem, see (Carroll, 2020)

so-called Boltzmann Brains – more frequently than they produce entire stable universes. Consequently, from a purely statistical standpoint, a randomly selected conscious observer seems more likely to be one of these ephemeral brains than a typical being with a coherent history in a large, consistent cosmos.

If it were genuinely more probable to be a Boltzmann Brain, then we would have no solid basis for trusting the continuity or stability of the reality we experience. Our memories, scientific laws, and any apparent evidence of a stable external universe could simply be momentary illusions without deeper meaning. This would undermine our confidence in observational data, making it exceedingly difficult to conduct science or trust in any form of knowledge.

However, from a theistic perspective – particularly an Islamic one – there is a notable advantage over a strictly naturalistic viewpoint. According to Islamic theism, God's creation is purposeful, not left to blind chance. The divine attributes of wisdom (*al-Ḥakīm*) and power (*al-Qādir*) ensure that genuine conscious life, intended for moral and spiritual development, prevails over Boltzmann Brains. Additionally, Islamic teachings on God's truthfulness and the reliability of revelation strengthen the credibility of our perceptions: if God created humans to recognize His signs in the universe (or multiverse), then a multitude of illusory observers would contradict that purpose. Consequently, fleeting brains with fabricated memories cannot outnumber real human observers.

It is not necessary to invoke a miracle that breaks the laws of nature to account for this. Even within a naturalistic framework, it is conceivable – though extremely unlikely – that the laws of physics would allow for extremely few or even zero Boltzmann Brains. In that sense, the situation parallels the fine-tuning argument discussed in the previous section. Consequently, under an Islamic framework, worries about Boltzmann Brains are greatly reduced or may not arise at all.

5 The Way of Love: Human Significance in a Vast Universe

The universe is vast beyond human imagination. As discussed in the first section, modern cosmology reveals a universe stretching across billions of light-years, filled with galaxies, stars, and potentially countless other life forms. This immensity often raises an unsettling question: How can human existence matter in the grand scheme of things? If we are merely a speck in an infinite expanse, does our presence hold any real significance? How can my few decades of life – or a humanity that is only a few hundred thousand years old – matter in a universe billions of years in age?

French philosopher Blaise Pascal captured this existential unease eloquently:

> When I consider the short duration of my life, swallowed up in an eternity before and after, the little space I fill, engulfed in the infinite immensity of spaces of which I know nothing, and which don't know anything of me, I am terrified. The eternal silence of these infinite spaces frightens me. (Pascal, 1941: 74)

Throughout history, many religious traditions have portrayed the cosmos as a meaningful, purpose-driven reality in which human beings occupy a unique and privileged position. However, some argue that this belief conflicts with the vast and seemingly indifferent universe described by modern cosmology.

This section will focus on the Muslim perspective on this question and examine whether this challenge threatens Islamic theism.

Why should human significance depend on the size and age of the universe or our relative place within it? Several philosophers have attempted to answer this question.

Guy Kahane argues that our sense of insignificance is tied to the abundance or rarity of intelligent life in the universe (Kahane, 2013). He contends that the sheer size of the universe is not what matters. Rather, if the universe is teeming with intelligent civilizations, then humans are not unique, and our significance diminishes. Conversely, if intelligent life is exceedingly rare, our significance increases, as we would represent a unique and extraordinary phenomenon. Just as gold is valuable because of its rarity and properties, human significance, in this view, depends on how common or replaceable we are in the cosmic scheme.

Nick Hughes, however, disagrees with Kahane (Hughes, 2017). He argues that humans feel insignificant not because of our rarity or commonness but due to our limited causal impact on the universe. The universe is vast, and human actions appear to have almost no effect on its overall workings. Our lives are temporary, and Earth itself is merely a tiny speck in an immense cosmos. This lack of causal power – the ability to shape or influence the larger universe – is what makes us feel small and unimportant.

Muslim responses to the question of human significance can stem from various schools of thought. However, due to space constraints, I will primarily focus on the Sufi perspective.[31] While a considerable number of Muslims – particularly *Salafis* – may not accept the full scope of Sufi metaphysics, I believe the general idea that human significance lies in one's relationship with God is widely shared.

Sufi metaphysics emphasizes that one's significance is not determined by physical size or impact, but rather by spiritual status and connection with the

---

[31] For an accessible introduction to Sufism intended for absolute beginners, one can consult (Chittick, 2007).

Divine. In other words, though human beings may be physically small, they possess immense spiritual depth and divine potential.

The Qur'an repeatedly describes the cosmos as a collection of *signs* (*āyāt*) pointing to God's existence and attributes:

> We will show them Our signs in the horizons and within themselves until it becomes clear to them that it is the truth. (*Fuṣṣilat* 41:53)

For Sufis – and Muslims in general – the universe is not an indifferent, meaningless expanse. It is a vast sign pointing to God's names and attributes. The renowned Sufi thinker Ibn 'Arabī teaches that everything in existence is a *manifestation* (*tajallī*) of God's names and attributes (Chittick, 2020). In this view, the vastness of the universe reflects God's infinite nature, not human insignificance.

Moreover, the Qur'an states that the creation of the universe is a greater feat than the creation of humankind, demonstrating God's immense power:

> Certainly, the creation of the heavens and the earth is greater than the creation of mankind, but most people do not know. (*Ghāfir* 40:57)

From this perspective, the feeling of smallness should not lead to nihilism but to humility and wonder – attitudes that fosters spiritual awakening. Humans must recognize that they are not in control of the universe; God is. In fact, according to Sufis and the two primary theological schools, the *Ash'arites* and *Māturīdīs*, humans do not possess a causal power at all, even in their immediate surroundings, let alone over galaxies.

Hughes's interpretation of insignificance stems from a misunderstanding – human purpose concerns the moral and spiritual, not the domination of the cosmos. In Islam, significance is redefined by separating it from physical impact and rooting it in consciousness, spiritual connection, and moral transformation. From this perspective, human worth is not determined by how much we can influence the universe on a physical level, but by our role as moral and spiritual beings whose actions resonate beyond time and space. This viewpoint is central to Sufi metaphysics, which emphasizes the inner world (spiritual reality) as more consequential than the outer world (material reality). In essence, spiritual transformation carries greater weight than material change.

Islamic thought teaches that even a single act of goodness – prayer, love, or the pursuit of knowledge – contains *barakah* (divine blessing) that transcends time and space. This is because humans are intimately connected to the ultimate cause that created and sustains the universe – God, who says in the Qur'an:

> We are closer to him [the human] than his jugular vein. (*Qāf* 50:16)

God's love is the key component extending human value beyond space and time. Ibn ʿArabi elaborates on this divine love while commenting on the Qur'anic verse, "And He is with you wherever you are" (*al-Ḥadīd* 57:4):

> God's love for His servants is not qualified by origin or end, for it does not accept qualities that are temporal or accidental ... Hence the relation of God's love to them is the same as the fact that He is with them wherever they are [57:4] ... Just as He is with them in the state of their existence, so also He is with them in the state of their nonexistence, for they are the objects of His knowledge. He witnesses them and loves them never endingly ... He has always loved His creatures, just as He has always known them ... His existence has no first point, so His love for His servants has no first point. (Ibn ʿArabī, n.d., vol. 2, 329.5)

The Qur'an teaches that human beings were entrusted with the *Amanah* (trust) of moral and spiritual responsibility:

> Indeed, We offered the Trust to the heavens and the earth and the mountains, and they declined to bear it and feared it; but man undertook to bear it. Indeed, he was unjust and ignorant. (*al-Aḥzāb* 33:72)

Unlike other creatures, humans possess free will, allowing them to choose between good and evil. This moral responsibility gives them significance. The Qur'an also states that God made humans His *vicegerents* (*Khalīfah*) on Earth:

> And [remember] when your Lord said to the angels, "Indeed, I will make upon the earth a vicegerent [Khalifah]." (*al-Baqarah* 2:30)

Human significance, therefore, comes from their influence and responsibility on Earth, not from their dominion over the entire universe. This perspective challenges Kahane's view – humans remain significant even if the universe is teeming with intelligent life.

It is also important to note that the Qur'an does not claim that humans are the most important species created by God:

> And We have certainly honored the children of Adam and carried them on land and sea and provided for them with good things and preferred them over much of what We have created, with [definite] preference. (*al-Isrāʾ* 17:70)

This verse suggests the possibility of other beings who may be superior to humans in certain ways. Nevertheless, human worth is not determined by the number of beings God has created but by their connection with and love for God.

If the universe's vastness is a sign intended for us, how should we interpret it? Sufis view physical smallness as a path to spiritual greatness. The immensity of the universe is not a cause for despair but a reminder of the illusory nature of ego and attachment to the self. By recognizing our smallness in the material realm, we can strive to become vast in the spiritual realm.

Fanā' (annihilation of the self) refers to dissolving one's ego in divine love, paradoxically making one more significant by drawing closer to God. This spiritual transformation is beautifully evoked by Rumi:

> I know nothing of that wine – I'm annihilated.
> I've gone too far into No-place to know where I am.
> Sometimes I fall to the depths of an ocean,
> then I rise up again like the sun.
> ...
> I can't be held by any place in the world,
> I know nothing but that placeless Friend. (Chittick, 2007: 116)

In this sense, smallness is liberating: it helps us relinquish our attachments to worldly concerns and become fully present with God. Sufis often link the following Qur'anic verse to the concept of *fanā'*:

> Everyone on it (the earth) will perish, but the Face of your Lord, full of Majesty and Honor, will remain. (*ar-Raḥmān* 55:26–27)

In fact, human smallness is a reminder of what Hughes identifies as the source of the problem: believing we must control everything. Embracing our smallness frees us from that illusion. The Islamic principle of *tawakkul* (trust in God) emerges from the recognition that we are not the ultimate controllers of reality.

Returning to Ibn 'Arabī's perspective: if human beings can achieve *fanā'*, they may attain the state of *al-Insān al-Kāmil* (the Perfect Man) (Chittick, 2020). In this state, humans become a "mirror" of the divine attributes or names, having cleansed themselves of the ego's "dirt." Thus, humans are greater than the universe in meaning and purpose because they can mirror divine names. The universe exists to facilitate knowledge of God, but human beings are capable of recognizing and reflecting God's names in their fullness.

From an Islamic, and especially a Sufi, viewpoint, human worth is not measured by physical size or cosmic influence but by the depth of one's spiritual connection to God. While modern cosmology may dwarf humanity in time and space, it also underscores the grandeur of a universe intended as a sign (*āyah*) pointing to the Divine. Our seeming smallness, far from rendering us insignificant, can awaken humility, dependence on God, and a sense of sacred responsibility as His *vicegerents* on Earth. This moral and spiritual responsibility – which includes recognizing and reflecting the divine names – defines our true stature. In Sufi thought, dissolving the ego (*fanā'*) and becoming a mirror of the divine attributes (*al-Insān al-Kāmil*) bestows a cosmic significance that transcends material limitations. Hence, human value emerges not from the ability to reshape the universe, but from the capacity to know, love, and reflect the One who created it.

This Element was meant to ponder our modern cosmological view, the signs of God in the cosmos – and perhaps within the boundless possibilities of a multiverse – so that we might glimpse, however faintly, the radiance of the Infinite. In doing so, we have traversed the delicate paths of reason and revelation, observing how the heavens invite us to marvel at a Creator whose majesty dwarfs our imagination, yet whose nearness warms our very souls. Thank you for accompanying me on this journey, and may our reflections continue to guide us toward deeper wonder and closeness to Reality (*Al-Ḥaqq*).

References

Adams, F., & Laughlin, G. (1999). *The Five Ages of the Universe*. New York: Simon & Schuster.

al-Ghazālī. (1993). *Kitāb al-Ḥikma fī Makhlūqāt Allāh*. Muḥammad Riḍā (Ed.). Beirut: Dār al-Kutub al-'Ilmiyya.

al-Ghazālī. (2000). *The Incoherence of the Philosophers / Tahâfut al-Falâsifa: A Parallel English-Arabic Text* (M. E. Marmura, Ed. & Trans., 2nd ed.). Provo, UT: Brigham Young University Press.

al-Ghazālī, M. (2001). *Faith in Divine Unity and Trust in Divine Providence* [Book 35 of *The Revival of Religious Sciences*]. Louisville, KY: Fons Vitae.

al-Ghazālī. (2013). *Moderation in Belief* (A. M. Yaqub, Trans.). Chicago, IL: University of Chicago Press.

al-Rāzī, F. (1987). *al-Maṭālib al-'āliya min 'ilm al-ilāhī* (Vol. 3). A. H. al-Saqqā (Ed.). Beirut: Dār al-Kitāb al-'Arabī.

Altaie, B. (2019). *The Divine Word and the Grand Design: Interpreting the Qur'an in the Light of Modern Science*. Manchester: Beacon Books.

Barnes, L. A. (2012). The fine-tuning of the universe for intelligent life. *Publications of the Astronomical Society of Australia*, 29(4), 529–564.

Barnes, L. A. (2018). Fine-tuning in the context of Bayesian theory testing. *European Journal for Philosophy of Science*, 8(2), 253–269.

Barrow, J. D., & Tipler, F. J. (1986). *The Anthropic Cosmological Principle*. Oxford: Clarendon Press.

Bradley, D. (2009). Multiple universes and observation selection effects. *American Philosophical Quarterly*, 46, 61–72.

Caro, H. D. (2020). *The Best of All Possible Worlds? Leibniz's Philosophical Optimism and Its Critics 1710–1755*. Leiden: Brill.

Carr, B., & Rees, M. (1979). The anthropic principle and the structure of the physical world. *Nature*, 278, 605–612.

Carroll, S. M. (2020). Why Boltzmann brains are bad. In S. Dasgupta, B. Weslake, & R. Dotan (Eds.), *Current Controversies in Philosophy of Science* (pp. 7–20). New York: Routledge.

Carter, B. (1974). Large number coincidences and the anthropic principle in cosmology. In M. S. Longair (Ed.), *Confrontations of Cosmological Theories with Observational Data (IAU Symposium, Vol. 63)* (pp. 291–298). Dordrecht: D. Reidel.

Chittick, W. C. (1989). *The Sufi Path of Knowledge: Ibn al-'Arabī's Metaphysics of Imagination*. Albany, NY: State University of New York Press.

Chittick, W. C. (2007). *Sufism: A Beginner's Guide*. Oxford: Oneworld.

Chittick, W. C. (2020). Ibn ʿArabī. In E. N. Zalta (Ed.), *The Stanford Encyclopedia of Philosophy (Spring 2020 ed.)*. https://plato.stanford.edu/archives/spr2020/entries/ibn-arabi/.

Clark, K. J. (2014). *Religion and the Sciences of Origins: Historical and Contemporary Discussions*. New York: Palgrave Macmillan.

Clegg, B. (2019). *Dark Matter and Dark Energy: The Hidden 95% of the Universe*. London: Icon Books.

Collins, R. (2003). Evidence for fine tuning. In N. Manson (Ed.), *God and Design: The Teleological Argument and Modern Science* (pp. 189–190). Abingdon: Routledge.

Collins, R. (2009). The teleological argument: An exploration of the fine-tuning of the universe. In W. L. Craig, & J. P. Moreland (Eds.), *The Blackwell Companion to Natural Theology* (pp. 202–281). Chichester: Wiley-Blackwell.

Collins, R. (2018). The argument from physical constants: The fine-tuning for discoverability. In J. L. Walls, & T. Dougherty (Eds.), *Two Dozen (or so) Arguments for God: The Plantinga Project* (pp. 89–107). New York: Oxford University Press.

Davidson, H. (1987). *Proofs for Eternity, Creation and the Existence of God in Medieval Islamic and Jewish Philosophy*. New York: Oxford University Press.

Davies, P. (1982). *The Accidental Universe*. New York: Cambridge University Press.

Davies, P. (1984). *God and the New Physics*. London: Penguin Books.

Davies, P. (2007). *The Goldilocks Enigma*. Boston, MA: Houghton Mifflin Harcourt.

Davies, P. C. W. (1983). The anthropic principle. *Progress in Particle and Nuclear Physics*, 10, 1–38.

Dawkins, R. (2008). *The God Delusion*. New York: Mariner Books.

Doko, E. (2019a). Criticism of the non-theistic explanations of fine-tuning. *Beytulhikme: An International Journal of Philosophy*, 9(9:2), 299–317. https://doi.org/10.18491/beytulhikme.1490.

Doko, E. (2019b). Does fine-tuning need an explanation? *Kader*, 17(1), 1–14. https://doi.org/10.18317/kaderdergi.552749.

Doko, E. (2024). Islamic theism and the multiverse. *Religions*, 15(7), 861. https://doi.org/10.3390/rel15070861.

Doko, E., & Turner, J. B. (2023). Islamic religious epistemology. In J. Fuqua, J. Greco, & T. McNabb (Eds.), *The Cambridge Handbook of Religious Epistemology* (pp. 148–162). Cambridge: Cambridge University Press.

Dorling, J. (1970). Dimensional analysis and the fine-tuning argument. *American Journal of Physics*, 38, 539.

Draper, P. (2004). Cosmic fine-tuning and terrestrial suffering: Parallel problems for theism and naturalism. *American Philosophical Quarterly*, 41, 311–321.

Ehrenfest, P. (1917). In what way does it become manifest in the fundamental laws of physics that space has three dimensions? *Proceedings of the Amsterdam Academy*, 20, 200–209.

Esed, M. (2002). *Kuran Mesajı: Meal-Tefsir*. İstanbul: İşaret.

Forrest, P. (1981). The problem of evil: Two neglected defences. *Sophia*, 20, 49–54.

Freeman, K., & McNamara, G. (2006). *In Search of Dark Matter*. New York: Springer.

Gould, P. (2011). The problem of God and abstract objects. *Philosophia Christi*, 13, 255–274.

Greene, B. (1999). *The Elegant Universe: Superstrings, Hidden Dimensions, and the Quest for the Ultimate Theory*. New York: W. W. Norton.

Greene, B. (2011). *The Hidden Reality: Parallel Universes and the Deep Laws of the Cosmos*. New York: Vintage.

Guessoum, N. (2011). *Islam's Quantum Question: Reconciling Muslim Tradition and Modern Science*. London: I. B. Tauris.

Guth, A. H. (1981). Inflationary universe: A possible solution to the horizon and flatness problems. *Physical Review D*, 23, 347–356.

Guth, A. (1997). *The Inflationary Universe: The Quest for a New Theory of Cosmic Origins*. New York: Basic Books.

Hacking, I. (1987). The inverse gambler's fallacy: The argument from design. The anthropic principle applied to Wheeler universes. *Mind*, 96(383), 331–340.

Hawking, S., & Mlodinow, L. (2010). *The Grand Design*. New York: Bantam Books.

Hogan, C. J. (2000). Why the universe is just so. *Reviews of Modern Physics*, 72(4), 1149–1161. https://doi.org/10.1103/RevModPhys.72.1149.

Hoover, J. (2004). Perpetual creativity in the perfection of God: Ibn Taymiyya's hadith commentary on God's creation of this world. *Journal of Islamic Studies*, 15(3), 287–329.

Howard-Snyder, D., & Howard-Snyder, F. (1994). How an unsurpassable being can create a surpassable world. *Faith and Philosophy*, 11, 260–268.

Hughes, N. (2017). Do we matter in the cosmos? *Aeon*. https://aeon.co/essays/just-a-recent-blip-in-the-cosmos-are-humans-insignificant.

Ibn ʿArabī. (n.d.). *Al-Futūḥāt al-Makkiyya*. Beirut: Dār Ṣādir.

Ibn Rushd. (1998). *Al-Kashf 'an Manahij al-Adillah fi 'Aqa'id al-Millah* (M. Hanafi, Ed.). Beirut: Center for Arab Unity Studies.

Ibn Sina. (1960). *Al-Shifā' al-Ilāhiyyāt*. G. Anawati & S. Zayed (Eds.). Cairo: Al-Hay'a.

Ibn Sina. (1968–1971). *Al-Ishārāt wa-l-Tanbīhāt*. S. Dunya (Ed.). Cairo: Dār al-Ma'ārif.

Ibn Sina. (2005). *The Metaphysics of The Healing* (M. E. Marmura, Ed. & Trans.). Provo, UT: Brigham Young University Press.

Ibn Taymiyyah. (1991). *Dar' Ta'āruḍ al-'Aql wa-l-Naql*, M. Rashād Sālim (Ed.). Riyadh: Jāmi'at al-Imām Muḥammad b. Sa'ūd al-Islāmiyya.

Ibn Taymiyyah. (1995). *Majmū' Fatāwā Shaykh al-Islām Aḥmad b. Taymiyya*, M. Rashād Sālim (Ed.). Riyadh: Dār al-'Ālam al-Kutub.

Jantzen, B. C. (2014). *An Introduction to Design Arguments*. Cambridge: Cambridge University Press.

Kahane, G. (2013). Our cosmic insignificance. *Noûs*, 47(2), 745–772. https://doi.org/10.1111/nous.12030.

Karaman, H., Çağrıcı, M., Dönmez, İ. K., & Gümüş, S. (2020). *Kur'an Yolu Türkçe Meâl ve Tefsir*. Ankara: Diyanet İşleri Başkanlığı.

Kraay, K. J. (2010). Theism, possible worlds, and the multiverse. *Philosophical Studies*, 147, 355–368.

Kragh, H. (2007). *Conceptions of Cosmos: From Myths to the Accelerating Universe: A History of Cosmology*. Oxford: Oxford University Press.

Laudan, L. (1981). A confutation of convergent realism. *Philosophy of Science*, 48(1), 19–49.

Leslie, J. (1989). *Universes*. London: Routledge.

Lewis, C. S. (2001). *Mere Christianity*. Harper One.

Lewis, D. (2001). *On the Plurality of Worlds*. Malden, MA: Blackwell.

Linde, A. D. (1983). Chaotic inflation. *Physics Letters B*, 129, 177–181.

Linde, A. (1994). The self-reproducing inflationary universe. *Scientific American*, 271(5), 48–55.

McGinnis, J. (2022). Simple is as simple does: Plantinga and Ghazālī on divine simplicity. *Religious Studies*, 58(S1), S97–S109.

McGinnis, J., & Acar, R. (2023). Arabic and Islamic philosophy of religion. In E. N. Zalta & U. Nodelman (Eds.), *The Stanford Encyclopedia of Philosophy* (Fall 2023 ed.). https://plato.stanford.edu/archives/fall2023/entries/arabic-islamic-religion/.

McGrew, T., McGrew, L., & Vestrup, E. (2001). Probabilities and the fine-tuning argument: A sceptical view. *Mind*, 110(440), 1027–1038.

Morris, T. V., & Menzel, C. (1986). Absolute creation. *American Philosophical Quarterly*, 23, 353–362.

Mukhanov, V. (2005). *Physical Foundations of Cosmology*. Cambridge: Cambridge University Press.

Mullā Ṣadrā. (2014). *The Book of Metaphysical Penetrations: A Parallel English-Arabic Text* (S. H. Nasr, Ed. & Trans.). Provo, UT: Brigham Young University Press.

Nasr, S. H., Dagli, C. K., Lumbard, J. E. B., & Rustom, M. (Eds.). (2015). *The Study Qur'an: A New Translation and Commentary*. New York: HarperOne.

Nicolson, I. (2007). *Dark Side of the Universe: Dark Matter, Dark Energy, and the Fate of the Cosmos*. Baltimore, MD: Johns Hopkins University Press.

North, J. (2008). *Cosmos: An Illustrated History of Astronomy and Cosmology*. Chicago, IL: University of Chicago Press.

Okuyan, M. (2024). *Kur'an: Meal-Tefsir*. İstanbul: Haliç Üniversitesi Yayınları.

Ormsby, E. L. (1984). *Theodicy in Islamic thought: The dispute over al-Ghazālī's "Best of all possible worlds."* Princeton, NJ:, Princeton University Press.

Öztürk, M. (2015). *Kuran ve Yaratılış*. İstanbul: Kuramer.

Page, D. N. (2008). Is our universe likely to decay within 20 billion years? *Physical Review D*, 78(6), 063535.

Parfit, D. (1998). Why anything? Why this? *London Review of Books*, 22, 24–27.

Pascal, B. (1941). *Pensées and the Provincial Letters*. New York: The Modern Library.

Penrose, R. (1989). *The Emperor's New Mind: Concerning Computers, Minds and Laws of Physics*. Oxford: Oxford University Press.

Penrose, R. (2004). *The Road to Reality*. London: Jonathan Cape.

Penrose, R. (2006). Before the big bang: An outrageous new perspective and its implications for particle physics. In *Proceedings of EPAC 2006* (10th European Particle Accelerator Conference), Edinburgh, UK, 26–30 June 2006. JACoW Publishing, Geneva, Switzerland (pp. 2759–2767).

Perlov, D., & Vilenkin, A. (2017). *Cosmology for the Curious*. Cham: Springer.

Plantinga, A. (1974). *God, freedom, and evil*. Grand Rapids, MI: Eerdmans.

Ragep, F. J. (2022). *Islamic Astronomy and Copernicus*. Ankara: Turkish Academy of Sciences.

Randall, L. (2005). *Warped Passages*. New York: HarperCollins.

Rees, M. (1999). *Just Six Numbers: The Deep Forces that Shape the Universe*. London: Weidenfeld & Nicolson.

Reichenbach, B. (1982). *Evil and a Good God*. New York: Fordham University Press.

Rowe, W. (1994). The problem of no best world. *Faith and Philosophy*, 11, 269–271.

Rubio, D. (2020). In defence of no best world. *Australasian Journal of Philosophy*, 98, 811–825.

Ryden, B. (2017). *Introduction to Cosmology* (2nd ed.). Cambridge: Cambridge University Press.

Saliba, G. (2007). *Islamic Science and the Making of the European Renaissance*. Cambridge, MA: MIT Press.

Schlesinger, G. (1977). *Religion and Scientific Method*. Dordrecht: Reidel.

Singh, S. (2005). *The Big Bang: The Origin of the Universe*. New York: Harper Perennial.

Smart, J. J. C. (1985). Laws of nature and cosmic coincidences. *The Philosophical Quarterly*, 35(140), 272–280.

Smart, J. J. C. (1989). *Our Place in the Universe: A Metaphysical Discussion*. Oxford: Blackwell.

Stanford, K. (2023). Underdetermination of scientific theory. In E. N. Zalta & U. Nodelman (Eds.), *The Stanford Encyclopedia of Philosophy* (Summer 2023 ed.). https://plato.stanford.edu/archives/sum2023/entries/scientific-underdetermination/.

Steinhardt, P. J., & Turok, N. (2004). The cyclic model simplified. *New Astronomy Reviews*, 49(2–6), 43–57.

Stenger, V. (2004). Is the universe fine-tuned for us? In M. Young, & T. Edis (Eds.), *Why Intelligent Design Fails: A Scientific Critique of the New Creationism* (pp. 172–184). New Brunswick, NJ: Rutgers University Press.

Stenger, V. (2011). *The Fallacy of Fine-Tuning: Why the Universe Is Not Designed for Us*. Amherst, NY: Prometheus Books.

Susskind, L. (2005). *The Cosmic Landscape: String Theory and the Illusion of Intelligent Design*. New York: Little, Brown.

Swinburne, R. (1979). *The Existence of God*. Oxford: Clarendon Press.

Tegmark, M. (1997). On the dimensionality of spacetime. *Classical and Quantum Gravity*, 14, L69–L75.

Tegmark, M. (2005). Parallel universes. *Scientific American*, 288, 40–51.

Tegmark, M., & Rees, M. (1998). Why is the cosmic microwave background fluctuation level 10^{-5}? *The Astrophysical Journal*, 499, 526–532.

Tegmark, M., Aguirre, A., Rees, M., & Wilczek, F. (2006). Dimensionless constants, cosmology, and other dark matters. *Physical Review D*, 73, 023505.

Tegmark, M. (2014). *Our Mathematical Universe: My Quest for the Ultimate Nature of Reality*. New York: Knopf.

Turner, D. A. Jr. (2003). The many universe solution of the problem of evil. In R. Gale & A. Pruss (Eds.), *The Existence of God* (pp. 1–17). Aldershot: Ashgate.

Weinberg, S. (1977). *The First Three Minutes: A Modern View of the Origin of the Universe*. New York: Basic Books.

Weinberg, S. (1987). Anthropic bound on the cosmological constant. *Physical Review Letters*, 59, 2607.

White, R. (2000). Fine-tuning and multiple universes. *Noûs*, 34(2), 260–276.

Yavuz, Y. Ş. (2012). Usûl-i selâse. *TDV İslâm Ansiklopedisi*, 42, 212. İstanbul: İSAM.

Zwiebach, B. (2009). *A First Course in String Theory* (2nd ed.). Cambridge: Cambridge University Press.

Acknowledgements

I thank Kelly James Clark, Nidhal Guessoum, Stefano Bigliardi, and the anonymous reviewer for their helpful comments on earlier drafts of this manuscript.

Cambridge Elements

Islam and the Sciences

Nidhal Guessoum
American University of Sharjah, United Arab Emirates

Nidhal Guessoum is Professor of Astrophysics at the American University of Sharjah, United Arab Emirates. Besides Astrophysics, he has made notable contributions in Science & Islam/Religion, education, and the public understanding of science; he has published books on these subjects in several languages, including *The Story of the Universe* (in Arabic, first edition in 1997), *Islam's Quantum Question* (in English in 2010, translated into several languages), and *The Young Muslim's Guide to Modern Science* (in English 2019, translated into several languages), numerous articles (academic and general-public), and vast social-media activity.

Stefano Bigliardi
Al Akhawayn University in Ifrane, Morocco

Stefano Bigliardi is Associate Professor of Philosophy at Al Akhawayn University in Ifrane, Morocco. He trained as a philosopher of science, has a PhD in philosophy from the University of Bologna, and has been serving in different positions at universities in Germany, Sweden, Mexico, and Switzerland. He has published a monograph and a general-public book on Islam and Science as well as dozens of articles (peer-reviewed and popular) on the subject and others. Since 2016, he has taught undergraduate courses on Islam and Science at Al Akhawayn University in Ifrane, Morocco.

About the Series

Elements in Islam and the Sciences is a new platform for the exploration, critical review and concise analysis of Islamic engagements with the sciences: past, present and future. The series will not only assess ideas, arguments and positions; it will also present novel views that push forward the frontiers of the field. These Elements will evince strong philosophical, theological, historical, and social dimensions as they address interactions between Islam and a wide range of scientific subjects.

Cambridge Elements⁼

Islam and the Sciences

Elements in the Series

Islam and Science: Past, Present, and Future Debates
Nidhal Guessoum and Stefano Bigliardi

Islam's Encounter with Modern Science: A Mismatch Made in Heaven
Taner Edis

Islam and Environmental Ethics
Muhammad Yaseen Gada

Islam, Causality, and Science: Perspectives on Reconciliation of Islamic Tradition and Modern Science
Özgür Koca

Muslim Women in Science, Past and Present
Elmira Akhmetova

Islam and Pseudoscience
Stefano Bigliardi

Islam and Modern Cosmology
Enis Doko

A full series listing is available at: www.cambridge.org/EISC

Printed by Integrated Books International,
United States of America